RETHINK EVERYTHING

KYLE DRAPER
BRIAN VIEAUX

Cover by Ric Dominic Zarate
Layout by Princess Hannah Arsenio

RETHINK
EVERYTHING

YOU 'KNOW' ABOUT BEING A NEXT GEN LOAN OFFICER

KYLE DRAPER
BRIAN VIEAUX

CONTENTS

SOCIAL MEDIA IS HERE TO STAY

TOP PRODUCER PERSPECTIVES

SERVING OTHERS WITH EDUCATION & ADVOCACY

AI, TECH & PROCESS FOR THE WIN

CLOSING

THANK YOU MESSAGE

Foreword

Just 10 months ago, I was reading the foreword from one of my mentors to my first book, "Rethink Everything You 'Know' About Social Media."

I would have never imagined that less than a year later, I'd be writing this foreword for my second book! Pure craziness...

How did we get here?

And better yet, why should you care?

When I wrote my first book last year, I had a vision for what the "Rethink Everything" brand could be. It could be the New Age "book for dummies" series where we bring in experts in different industries to help the reader "rethink" what they assume they already know.

This book is that vision coming to life!

On the following pages, you'll experience 39 experts from the mortgage industry who have left all of themselves in this book.

They want the mortgage industry to grow.
They want mortgage companies to flourish.
They want the consumer to be highly educated and served.

You're about to experience a book like never before.

You'll find insight in each chapter, QR codes to videos from the authors, and even drawings to keep it fun and engaging.

Open your mind, be willing to accept some hard truths, and experience growth in your business like never before.

PS - If you think you have a book in you…maybe it's time you help people "Rethink Everything." Let's chat!

Thank you to the men and women who so selflessly wrote these pages. Your willingness to bear all is an encouragement to where our industry is headed.

KYLE DRAPER

INTRODUCTION

A Next Gen Loan Officer is uniquely positioned to be the **MOST TRUSTED** resource for financial education and preparation for the next generation of homebuyers.

Why do I believe this?

The typical early journey first time home buyer has not yet accumulated enough assets to be on the radar of a financial advisor. For a lot of them, the ATM or banking app on their phone is their private banker.

So where do they turn when beginning their home buying journey? Most rely on the internet. And more specifically, social media. Younger millennials and older Gen Zers use TikTok, YouTube and Instagram as their first stop on this learning journey. They follow financial influencers 'finfluencers', some of whom are Loan Officers, to understand what they need to do to become a successful homeowner.

The next generation homebuyer is distinctly different from prior generations in many ways. Where they learn and how they consume information is one of the biggest differences. Loan Officers, of all ages and across all channels, need to better understand this future homebuyer cohort if they are to remain relevant and have any chance of future success.

This book is not a technical "how to" manual on being a loan officer. Rather, it is a collaboration of like minded professionals across the industry, representing different roles, who have selflessly shared their experience and knowledge, with the sole objective of helping you, our reader, the Next Gen Loan Officer.

The book is much more than just 'words on a page'. You are invited, throughout the book, to go a layer deeper and "meet" the experts. Other books, especially textbooks, are best consumed without distractions (ie: your phone). Not this one. Your phone is the portal to immerse yourself in the content and become part of this community. Connect with and engage the experts and build relationships that you never would in another type of book.

Scan the QR codes and discover even more than what was written. But don't stop there. We want this book to become a community. Connect with the writers, engage them on their socials, ask them questions about their chapter.

Let's give it a try.

In the sections and chapters that follow you are going to be exposed to ideas, philosophies, maybe even tools that will help you be more successful for years to come. It is ultimately up to you to decide what you will do with the information. The book is laid out in 6 sections, with 4-6 chapters each. Each section will give multiple perspectives and ideas on the topics. Again, it's up to you to decide which to align with your business and how you will employ.

One last thought before you get started. A Next Gen Loan Officer does not imply 'young'. 'Next Gen' is not about age, but rather mindset. Whether 25, 65, or any age between, you can be successful with the next generation of homebuyers. You simply need to show up and be where they are and be willing to be a teacher first.

Ready for it?

Let's Go!!!

BRIAN VIEAUX

brian.vieaux@finlocker.com

Presented by:

In this opening section "Mindset Matters," you are invited on a journey through the intricate world of mindset reshaping, tailored for the next-gen loan officer.

With chapters penned by industry titans, this section will go deep into the pivotal role of attention to detail, the power of being a difference-maker, fostering solid relationships, bridging the gap between intentions and execution, and leveraging modern recruiting strategies. These narratives emphasize that success in the mortgage industry goes well beyond mere knowledge and skills; it's fundamentally rooted in cultivating a growth mindset, embracing failure as a steppingstone, and persistently striving for personal and professional evolution. Through real-world insights and actionable strategies, loan officers will be equipped to navigate the complexities of their roles with confidence, innovation, and a deep understanding of the human element at the heart of every transaction.

CHAPTER 1:

The Mortgage Game: Learning from Brown M&Ms

Looking back on my career in the mortgage industry, one truth has become crystal clear: success in this game lies in following a process and paying attention to the details, from understanding a borrower's needs to planning out my day. As I reflect on my over two-decade journey, I can point to many instances where our industry and one of my favorite stories come together.

Legendary rock band Van Halen had a somewhat odd backstage request to remove all brown M&Ms from the backstage area. Turns out, it wasn't just rockstar vanity. Van Halen included the M&M request as a test for event organizers. It ensured the promoters read the safety details in their contract. An overlooked piece of candy can teach a valuable lesson: paying attention to the little details can be the difference between a smooth deal and potential problems—in rock and roll or mortgage origination.

When it comes to mortgage, I want to share some important areas I feel a loan officer needs to focus on when it comes to details.

CUSTOMER EXPERIENCE AND FOLLOW-UP

Beware of falling into a trap I've seen so many originators end up in. The focus is mainly on the outcome and with all the excitement of getting a loan, you fail to give the customer a great experience. More importantly, you don't have a strategy in place for following up throughout the experience. Your database is your biggest asset; if you have a good follow-up plan, it will set you apart and help you get more referrals.

Think of the best (or worst) customer experience you've received. Maybe it's when you applied for your first mortgage, went car shopping, or on vacation. How was your experience from beginning to end? List five things from that experience that made it good or bad. Now, compare your experience to your process. Are you leaving anything out? What can you do better or more often?

Here are the steps to create a great customer experience whether it's a new lead, an existing customer, or a closed customer. As you read, think about your process. Do you have a consistent plan or are you lacking in a certain area that needs improvement?

Step 1: Initial Lead

- What happens when you get a lead?
- What do you do on day one, two, or five? How long until you reach out? What is your method of contact? What do you talk about?

Step 2: Post-conversion

- How does your customer service journey change once you convert the lead?
- Do you have a follow-up plan?
- How often are you reaching out and what are you sharing?

Step 3: Post-closing

- Do you follow up in 30 days to see if everything is going well knowing that's when they will have the most questions?
- Do you check in twice a year, including a phone call on the anniversary of their closing?
- Do you send a birthday card?

Step 4: Create Surprise

- Incorporate at least three surprises into the overall journey.
- People tend to remember how we make them feel more than what we say.
- Take the time to show them that you value them.

DATA

I have a love-hate relationship with data. It never lies and it's never emotional. To me, data is a lot like the weight scale. If you're trying to lose weight, you need to track your progress. Some days you've gained weight, and you look back and say, "Why did I gain weight? What did I do different? And some days you lose weight, and you ask yourself those same questions. Just as tracking daily progress is essential for weight loss, in the mortgage business, consider what key metrics you should be monitoring.

Leads, Conversion Rate, and Closed Rate

- How many leads are you getting?
- What is your conversion rate?
- What is your closed rate?

Leads Source Analysis

- Where are you getting your leads from?
- Where do you need to improve in getting more leads in certain areas? I found that many originators say, "I'm getting 30 leads, I'm getting 40 leads." But then they never go back into the data of where those leads are coming from. Is there an area where you're weak at and need to improve?

CALENDAR

While customer service, follow-up, and data are crucial details to pay attention to, none of them will work if your calendar isn't in line. When I'm designing my calendar, I split it into three areas:

Green: Selling & connecting
- Specific time for engaging with clients and driving sales.

Red: Operational Responsibilities
- Handle operational tasks and responsibilities.

Blue Time: Vision Planning (what's next)
- Allocate time for strategic planning—whether in recruiting, refining sales processes, or exploring new software. It's a critical investment to elevate your origination business. Many successful loan officers neglect to plan for what's next, missing opportunities for growth.

ENCORE, ENCORE, ENCORE···

Success in mortgages goes beyond checking off boxes; it's about paying attention to the details that create something worth cheering for. Using your inner Van Halen, you can approach each day with a unique perspective and a commitment to extreme follow-up.

In this business, finding the equivalent of a brown M&M is the secret to winning—prioritize the little things, and watch the big things unfold!

CHAPTER 2:
Being a Difference-maker

One of the greatest blessings in my career is that I have had a chance to train and coach thousands of top performers across the country. And when I say top, I'm talking $100M, $200M and $300M+ producers. And after 41 years of managing, coaching, and training well over a million loan officers, I have identified a handful of universal traits of top performers. In this chapter I want to cover one of the most common: being a difference-maker.

Zig Ziglar said, "When it comes to new customers, we treat them in one of two ways; like a prospect or a suspect." Sadly, the latter of these is, by far, the most common that I see in our industry.

With the proliferation of technology (specifically digital applications and automated communication) and historic low rates, the fact is that most loan officers, post-pandemic, are simply order-takers, not difference-makers.

And although they may have been able to get away with that in the lowest rate market in history, loan officers simply will not be able to in a traditional rate market.

To truly separate themself in any market and achieve top performance consistently—regardless of rates—a loan officer simply must be a difference-maker. So let me share a few proven and killer strategies that have helped loan officers across the country blow their sales through the roof!

The first step is eliminating three critical mistakes most loan officers make when starting conversations with their leads and referrals.

MISTAKE #1:
Treating borrowers like suspects, not prospects

The most common mistake loan officers make is opening with qualifying questions right up-front with no conversation, personal connection, or value proposition. Most loan officers want to get right to the point. They don't want to waste their time (or the borrower's, so they say), so they lead with qualifying questions. For purchases, most loan officers jump straight into questions about how expensive of a home the borrower is looking to buy, how much they want to put down, and their credit score and income. For refinances, most loan officers immediately ask what their existing home is worth, how much they owe, and their credit score and income. Of the more than 400 recorded sales calls I listened to in 2023, over 90% asked these kinds of questions in the first minute or two of the call.

Some may ask, *"What's the problem with that?"*

Simple: if a loan officer starts with these kinds of questions, the message they are conveying to their borrowers is: "If you are good enough, I will spend time with you. If not, I won't." With that kind of message, is the borrower being treated as a prospect or suspect? You decide.

MISTAKE #2:
Focusing On Price and Product

I see it all the time, loan officers quote rate, in some form or fashion, within the first few minutes of the call—before they have any semblance of relationship, credibility, trust, curiosity, or value developed. They reference closing costs, escrows, buy-downs and lender credits. They talk about FHA, VA, conforming, and USDA, as if most borrowers have a clue what they are talking about! The reality is that most borrowers think par is a golf term and that a USDA is a steak.

In most cases, focusing on price and product prematurely kills sales. Why? First off, doing so arms borrowers with exactly what they need to shop the market—a critical mistake in the most competitive market in history! Between online rate quotes, credit triggers, and media, when loan officers start with price and product, they are giving their competition rates, fees and products to compare to and beat.

Additionally, a price and product focus subconsciously communicates to borrowers that the rate is the most important element of a mortgage. If that's true, here's the problem every price-focused loan officer faces: there is always a lower rate out there. The fact is that there are thousands of lenders in the U.S. alone, and only one of them has the lowest at any given moment. Which makes the odds of any loan officer being able to truly offer the lowest rate impossible.

But even if a loan officer can offer a borrower the lowest possible rate, the minute that customer is given the opportunity to shop the competition, there's no question what most lenders' answer will be to whether they can beat it: *"Yes!"*

MISTAKE #3:
Talking Mortgages, Not Money

Let me share an absolute truth: as an originator, your product is not mortgages, it's money! At the end of the day, every borrower is looking for the same two things: how they can save money (that's why they always start with asking about the rate), and how they can get money (whether to purchase a home, build wealth, make improvements to their existing home, eliminate debt, etc.). What most loan officers focus on is the type of mortgages they offer, their process, guidelines, turn times, etc. While these do all have to be discussed at some point, they should never be the first or primary focus of the call.

All these mistakes lead to transactional, non-emotional, confusing, and boring order-taking. So, how can loan officers move away from being order-takers and elevate their game to become difference-makers? Let me offer these suggestions:

DIFFERENCE-MAKER HABIT #1:
Start with Appreciation

Whether connecting with a lead or referral, next-generation loan officers start every call with sincere appreciation. They let their borrowers know—right out of the gate—how grateful they are for the opportunity to serve them. They let their borrowers know that, whether a past customer, referral, or simply someone that inquired through a website or responded to a marketing effort, their business is not taken for granted and that they intend to earn it!

Next-generation loan officers spend time really digging into what their borrowers are looking to do. They don't just ask about the immediate need or the purpose of the loan but go deeper into everything their borrowers want to accomplish through a mortgage. They take time to discern what really matters to their borrowers and to understand their expectations for every aspect of the process.

Having ascertained a complete understanding of their borrowers' goals, desires, and expectations, next-generation loan officers take time to quickly credential themselves and their company. Why? To give their borrowers confidence that they are the right loan officer to prioritize what matters to them and solve their needs through a mortgage.

Lastly, next-generation loan officers find ways to connect with their borrowers on a personal level. They don't just ask questions for the sake of asking questions, but listen attentively, repeat back their borrowers' stated needs, and respond empathetically to their emotions.

DIFFERENCE-MAKER HABIT #2:
Keep the Rule of 5s

Next-generation loan officers understand that attempting to answer the rate question up-front is not just deadly, but impossible. There's simply no way to know what a borrower's rate is going to be without first knowing everything about them. When originators quote a rate up-front, prior to getting enough information to fully understand the borrower's situation, qualifications, and goals (in other words: a complete application), they're guessing with 100% inaccuracy.

To quote an accurate rate, an originator must know more than just their borrowers' basic qualifications. They need to understand their borrowers' complete financial situations and goals to first identify the right products, terms, programs, and loan configurations. Without having identified those, a quoted rate is nothing more than a meaningless number.

In contrast to quoting rates up-front, next-generation loan officers gain a deep understanding of their borrowers' needs and desires. Then they craft a value statement built on what I call the Rule of 5s, which states that a customer is significantly more likely to buy a product or service when presented with five tangible benefits of doing so.

Applied to mortgages, the Rule of 5s demands that originators give every borrower five unique reasons why they and their company should be chosen over anyone else. Loan officers who have not sat down to identify and define their five unique reasons should do so immediately.

And then they should practice taking no more than 30 seconds to articulate their five reasons to every single borrower they interact with.

DIFFERENCE-MAKER HABIT #3:
Be a Money-giver-awayer

Next-generation loan officers understand their product is money and talk about it! They take time to educate their borrowers on the solutions they provide to deliver the three things everyone wants from their mortgage: savings, security, and stability.

For example, a next-generation loan officer might explain to a borrower how they are going to save them money by getting them into a lower payment through a refinance, or ensure they take on an affordable payment through a purchase. They might explain to a borrower how they are going to help them increase their wealth, liquidity, or appreciation. They might explain how they can work-up different down payment options to help them to retain more reserves or create more assets. They might explain to them how they can align their term with their long-term goals or shorten it to save them tens of thousands in interest.

In essence, next generation loan officers are committed to demonstrating to their borrowers how they are, as I love to say, money-giver-awayers!

BONUS TIP

Becoming a next-generation loan officer requires learning how to slow down. Deep relationships aren't developed quickly— they require accumulating a deep understanding of borrowers' long- and short-term goals.

Next-generation loan officers take the time that's needed to truly earn their customers' business. They provide such an unmatched experience it not only makes their competition look bad in comparison, but creates customers-for-life!

If you want to be a next-generation loan officer, start with becoming a difference-maker, a life-changer, and a money-giver-awayer!

CHAPTER 3:
The Value Gap

I am a recruiting coach who, over the past 7 years, has invested more than 12,000 hours coaching top leaders who are building teams to get extraordinary results. And I mean extraordinary!

When people think of recruiting, they think of phone scripts, making many calls, and dealing with hang-ups and rejection.

But that's not what I coach to. Because I want results, I want lifelong relationships with people who know me as a person who gives value before I ever ask for value in return. What I have been able to prove in my journey, as well as many others, is this: the more value we bring, the more in demand we become.

Now, take the idea of value and insert digital.

Whether you are recruiting realtors, buyers, loan officers, or anyone else, you must understand that the device you are holding right now OR have sitting within arms distance **is not a phone!** Yes, the phone is one of the apps on your smartdevice, but it is not the primary one where people are investing their time. Over the past five years, time on social media has risen to 2.5 hours per day. That data should have you building a plan to use social media in a big way to achieve your recruiting wins.

For decades, we have discussed the "6 degrees of separation" (a concept set by Frigyes Karinthy in 1929) and how it applies to business. But with the maturity of social media, there is NO degree of separation today.

Here is a simple plan as proof.

If you were to build a Dream 100 list of the top people you wanted to recruit and found them on social media, nothing would stop you from connecting with them and bringing them value.

I teach a framework of 4C's (a play on my company name, 4C Recruiting) as a way to do this.

Connection: Find the individual on social media and follow/connect with them.

Content: Create daily content that is centered around your five personas. What are the top things that best represent you? For me, it's…

1) Husband
2) Father to 4 children
3) Outdoorsman who loves to fish and hunt
4) Recruiting coach
5) Recruiting consultant/strategist

Communicate: Engage with these people through your news feeds and inbox. Bring value before you ever ask for anything in return. The Law of Reciprocity states that if you bring enough value, people feel inclined to return the value.

Conversion: Bring value three times and then ask for a non-recruiting 15-minute meeting to get to know them for the future.

The key to success is committing to all 4Cs, not just conversion. Too many people see social media as a hack to get what they want, which is a connection that brings them value. It's why most people believe social media doesn't work for business because that's how they treat the platform. Then they get ghosted because no one wants to receive spam messages selling them.

Ideas are crap without execution so let's activate all of this with urgency to get you results.

Here is a way to execute this plan over the next 30 days.

1. Build a list of the top 100 people you want to recruit. Call it your Dream 100 list. Now, find every one of their social media channels.

2. Connect and follow them on social media.

3. Create daily content that they would find valuable. For example, my audience is leaders leading a team while recruiting top recruits to their teams. So here are some of the items I share.
   - Dos and don'ts of recruiting.
   - Research around recruiting helps them do more of the right things.
   - Recent conversations I have had where insightful topics have come up.
   - Any framework that simplifies recruiting.

4. Invest 15 minutes a day communicating with your Dream 100. Engage with their content. Share their content. If they aren't creating content, you can engage with their inbox by sharing items that they would find valuable. DO NOT create noise by sharing items they wouldn't be interested in. We are drowning in noise today BUT starving for real value.

5. On day 21, think like a journalist and go find something of real value for their business that you can share. I have found some fantastic gems over the years doing research. One of the best interviews I found was with Gary Vee and Tom Ferry, discussing the top ideas agents should apply to their business. Because it was hosted on someone else's YouTube channel, it only had a few hundred views. But the 30 minutes they shared was worth more than most people get from paid coaching.

6. Every 5 to 7 days, show up and bring tremendous value until you have sent three things.

7. Ask for a non-recruiting meeting. Here is a simple framework for this ask.

   - Affirm them from your research that leads you to believe they are amazing.

   - Give them a big reason why you are asking them for a meeting. An example of this is "the industry is changing dramatically." Be prepared to share why you believe that is.

   - Invite them into a 15-minute meeting where if they say yes, no recruiting allowed, simply getting to know each other for the future because if something changes in their career and/or business, you would be honored to receive a call one day.

This strategy works for anyone looking to recruit someone to their business and/or team. Here is why. It creates what I call

"THE VALUE GAP"

Here is my definition of the Value Gap: The distance created by someone with a strong core value system, which leads to them bringing value to people before they ask for anything of value.

If you want this to be your best year yet, create your value gap. You control every part of this, and when you focus on what you control, well, passion follows. Passionate people are great recruiters because recruiting is simply a transference of passion.

Now, get to it!

CHAPTER 4:
Between Intention and Execution

1) Create a written plan.

Abundant evidence tells us that writing out what you want to accomplish creates a bridge between what you want to do and what actually gets done.

I'm a big fan of the one-page business plan. For 20 years, I utilized the ***Building Champions Focus Plan***

(Scan the QR Code).

This plan consists of 4 elements;

Central Theme
Identify a theme for this season of life that will motivate you to stick to your plan.

Goals
Identify 3-4 things you really want to accomplish during this time period.

Disciplines
Build clear, actionable, and realistic disciplines into your daily routine that will help you hit your goals.

Projects
Identify worthwhile projects that will enhance the way you lead your personal and professional life.

 If you would like to go a bit deeper in your planning, I love *Gino Wickman's "Vision/ Traction Organizer" (V/TO)*

This tool helps you to identify what drives you and what will keep you connected to your daily schedule and disciplines.

Core Values
    Passions
    10-Year Target
    Lifetime Wish List

And then...

    Your 1-Year Plan
    Your "Rocks" (90-Day Goals)
    Issues List (Ideas, Problems, Obstacles)

Whether you utilize one of these tools, another refenced in this book or something completely different...

Go someplace where you won't be interrupted.

Write It Out.

2) Review it DAILY.

I know, because I've heard clients respond this way hundreds of times... "I wrote it, why do I have to review it?"

Because you want this indelibly written in your brain. It needs to become a part of you, ingrained in the way that you show up for your day.

When I was learning to fly, emergency procedures were to be memorized so that if the engine (the only engine) quit, I would know exactly what to do;

☑ Airspeed - 122 MPH
☑ Landing Site - Select
☑ Fuel Selector - Fullest Tank
☑ Mixture - Rich
☑ Aux Fuel Pump - On
☑ Mags - check L/R or Both

In a similar way, create your plan so that it guides your actions... EVERY SINGLE DAY.

3) Non-Negotiable Daily Disciplines By Noon

Commit to knocking out the 3 things that will move the needle for you (Annual Mortgage Review Calls, Social Media posting/engagement etc) **BY NOON**.

Parkinson's Law states that "a task will take the time available for its completion." So, rather than let the day unfold with the non-critical urgencies that will surely come your way, forcing you to give in at 3:45 in the afternoon, admitting that you didn't get them done... again. Commit.

 If I coached you, the first thing I'd have you do would be to order the "Win By Noon" planner. (This QR code will lead you to it.)

Whether you use Outlook, an app or a yellow pad – try this system for 90 days. If you commit to the basics of this system, it will change your productivity. *I guarantee it.*

4) Accountability with a coach.

Holding yourself accountable is challenging for most. We let ourselves off the hook. We rationalize. We lie to ourselves.

Having a coach that will hold you to what you have said you will do is imperative. (side note: IMO, it's not about what THEY tell you need to do, because then you won't own it. You decide and then let them hold you to it).

Fight deflection. This is such a common issue in coaching, that it's worth calling out. As a loan officer, you're in Sales, and as such, you know how to influence. When you feel yourself trying to get out of being held accountable by your coach by inserting an urgent "Coach, I really need to talk to you about this other thing," know that you are likely deflecting. *Stop it.*

5) Block Out Distractions.

Oh man. Here we go. For some of you, this is going to be really, really hard.

At any given time, dozens of things are fighting for your attention. Pop ups want your email address and phone number for that discount you might use, ads want your atention, co-workers want you to respond to them and friends want you to talk to them. Not to mention the UPS driver at the door and the phone ringing, the washing machine pinging and the dog that wants to go for a walk.

Constant notifications and text messages are every loan officer's enemy. Put your phone on silent or in "Do Not Disturb" mode, and close unnecessary tabs on your computer. If you need the Internet, keep one tab open. You can fight online distractions by blocking or hiding time-wasting websites and apps.

Noise cancelling headphones are an enormous help. Choose what works best for you; music that fuels your soul (without lyrics), focus music or white noise can all work. Experiment. For me, it's soft jazz or classical music at 60 beats per minute. Research and experiment here as everyone's different.

When writing my book, "White Collar Warrior – Lessons for Sales Professionals From America's Military Elite," I would schedule 90-minutes of writing, followed by a reward; driving range time or picking up a Jamba Juice worked for me.

The secret is to not experience the reward until you've done the work.

OK folks, if you want to move from I INTEND to do this, to I EXECUTED this… I've laid out my best stuff.

It's now up to you.

Start by scheduling at least 90-minutes to build that plan. Tell those that need to know, to help protect you from interruptions and go build a path to your better future!

CHAPTER 5:
Mindset 1st

One of my very first mentors gave me a piece of advice that has stuck with me for over 20 years. He said, *"The 11th Commandment is: Thou Shalt Not Foolith Thy Selfith."* In other words, don't fool yourself into believing something that's not true.

In the mortgage industry, we tend to fool ourselves a lot. We believe certain things are important when they aren't, and we think there's a perfect strategy we need to have to win and there's not. We convince ourselves that there are outside influences keeping us from achieving our goals, but like the title of this book, we have to **Rethink Everything!**

I've spent 20 years in the mortgage industry as a Loan Officer, Branch/Area Manager, Regional Vice President, and National Director. Over the last 5 years I've also been fortunate enough to have a successful podcast called Mortgage Marketing Expert, that helps mortgage pros build more modern and relevant businesses. Today, as the Founder of M1 Academy, I get to coach hundreds of mortgage and real estate professionals from dozens of companies and speak on stages all over the U.S. I don't share any of that looking for a pat on the back; I share it because these experiences have allowed me to collaborate with, and learn from, some of the best of the best in the mortgage business. I've been able to see firsthand what it takes to succeed, and it has very little to do with the tactics. It has much more to do with—

MINDSET

Mindset is not the only thing that's important, but it is the MOST important thing. Mindset controls our attitude and our actions, which are the only two things that we can actually control. We can't control clients, partners, companies, or the market; but we can control what we do and how we respond to things. Through thousands of hours as a coach, sales leader, and podcast host, I've identified specific things that some of the successful mortgage professionals have in common. I want to share a few of those with you here. You can find more of those principles in my upcoming book, *What the Uncommon Have in Common.*

The first trait that highly successful people have in common is:

They have a growth mindset that actually embraces it. Growing up in school, academia taught us that success is on one side, failure is on the other, and we have to decide which way we want to go. We couldn't fail every test and still be considered successful in that class, even if we learned everything we got wrong. We still failed; we were a failure. That's not how it works in the real world. Success and failure are not on opposite sides. Failure is on the path to success. In business we can fail over and over and still succeed, as long as we use the failure as an opportunity to learn. Nearly every high performer that I've spoken with has failed numerous times, often pointing to those failures as launching points that propelled them forward.

The next characteristic highly successful people have in common is:

They understand what people pay for.

People pay for solutions to their problems. Read that again. If you provide a solution to a problem or challenge that someone has in their life, they will pay you with their time, attention, loyalty, and yes, their money. The concept itself isn't that difficult to understand, but many mortgage professionals have the wrong perspective. What they think is a valuable solution often isn't what their clients and partners think is valuable. Also, many of those clients and partners are not actually aware of what problems they need solved. This disconnect shows the importance of conversations with open-ended questions rather than having a focus on selling your product or service. You are not in the mortgage business, you are in the happiness business.

Your job is to help people buy a home where they can create memories with their family or create a strategy to help them achieve their financial goals so that they can live a happy and fulfilling life. Make no mistake, solving that problem will create more results in your business than any other.

The final principle that I'll share here that all highly successful people have in common is:

They understand the importance of DIGITIZING their reputation into a personal brand.

Having a personal brand is talked about a lot, but we need to rethink what a personal brand really is. It's about the person, not the brand. The biggest corporations in the world pay celebrities, athletes, and personalities to personify their brand, because consumers can't create relationships with a company or a logo like they can an individual.

Ironically, the mortgage industry is a perfect example of clients deciding their mortgage provider based on the person they work with over the company itself. However, many mortgage professionals try to create a schtick or logo that looks and sounds like a big company. People care more about who you are than what you do. So, if you're not building a personal brand based off your personality, hobbies, experiences, and sharing content that showcases all of that, then you're missing out on the biggest opportunities you have to create connections with potential clients.

The higher the requirement for trust in a profession, the more important it is to have a personal brand.

The easiest way to create trust with someone is to find things in common with them. We are naturally drawn to and have an element of trust with people that are like us. The way to do that is by sharing content on social media about who you are, not just what you do.

In closing, I'll leave you with a bonus trait. The same highly successful people and elite performers I've been talking about will rarely allow themselves to believe that they are successful or elite. They are always trying to expand their mind, better themselves through daily disciplines, and take action to take their business to the next level.

Whenever they get close to achieving a goal, they push the goal even higher so that they have a reason to push themselves even further. Ask yourself, are you doing those things too? Are you building a bulletproof mindset? Are you taking action on a daily basis to move the needle toward your goals? Success in business, and in life, is about consistent and persistent effort over time. My challenge to you is to rethink the actions you take and how you respond to things, because that mindset is ultimately going to determine where your path goes.

Listen to the
Mortgage Marketing Expert podcast

Get a copy of
What the Uncommon Have in common

CHAPTER 6:
The Realtor Perspective

OK, so Kyle Draper is one of those people that when he calls and asks you to participate in something or to take action, I've figured out I should probably pay attention...aka *listen up*!

So I momentarily decided in late 2023 to take my advice and listen to what coach Kyle asked of me, which was, hey, "Do you want to write the chapter for my new book from a Realtors perspective." So I said yes and was quickly followed by Why me, which was again followed by, "Oh, everyone else must've said no." However, he responded, "I couldn't think of anyone better than you that would be transparent, give an honest perspective, and not hold back, so here we are. One more story before I share: the Mark perspective.

Relationships matter; more context later.

Let's get it over with and out in the open. I've heard for too long that Realtors drive Lenders crazy, and Lenders drive Realtors crazy. OK, we're good now. So stop saying this about Realtors because what you speak becomes what you believe, and what you think becomes your reality, and who the heck wants to exist in that career reality? Alright, let's say it together three times: I Love Realtors, I Love Realtors, I Love Realtors. Ok, ok, ok, let's say it a fourth because I know it's hard to believe; I Love Realtors.

Everything I have in life that is calculable is from a relationship that, for the most part, arrived from me doing something beneficial for someone else 1st. And the best Lender/Realtor partnership I've built to this day over 19 years into my Realtor journey, which lasted over a decade...is no different. Let's call him Sam for the sake of picking a name. He is the most all-in, service-minded, do-whatever-it-takes LO I have still met in the business to this day...I'll give you the 'Why' in a moment. Although we don't refer business back and forth any longer, I still have a fondness for the way he approached and handled both mine and my brokerage clients to this day. I don't remember who sent a referral 1st, but someone told him there was this new agent you have to meet, so she invited us both to the same bar; we shared a drink, decided we would like to 'try a deal together,' and the remainder of the next decade-plus, I swatted away any all attempts to do business with any other loan officers.

Alright, here we go...so you want those big hitters, laying it down, hustling, going all-in, whatever it takes no matter what attitude, intelligent, committed to me exclusively (cause, let's be honest, you wonder why you didn't receive their last referral when seeing the latest closing photo with another LO), Top performer, content creator, energetic, upbeat, problem-solving

Realtor to partner with. So does everyone else. Those are the unicorns!

And because the 1st state that I sold property in as a Realtor was the Great State of Kentucky, let's talk about horses & unicorns.

Alright, so you want a unicorn, and so does everyone. The 1st rule of Unicorns Realtors & LO's: If you want one, you must be one. Sam was one of these. Unicorns don't want to breed with normal horses because there is a 50/50 chance they would bare a horse baby, and unicorns only wish to bare unicorns. The good news is, *you can become a unicorn lender, and there is no better time than today to begin; it's time to start NOW.*

 We attract what we put out and usually nothing more, minus a lucky call once or twice. No one deserves anything but an equal chance, so wake up tomorrow and start living the life of a unicorn LO, living up to your similar expectations of those top Realtors when referring your family members' listing or purchase.

Be the loan officer you would hire. Take a moment to reflect on what you, the consumer, would desire from a loan officer today. Be that, nothing less, not 80% or 90% or even 99%....you gotta be 100% of the person you would hire, Nothing less. Anything less, and congratulations you're going to live a pleasant life as a grazing out to pasture LO. And just because someone will have their feelings hurt with this...out to pasture, isn't referring to age. Out to pasture means you just aren't willing to do Unicorn things.

If this seems too complicated or too tall of a mountain to climb and doesn't sound appealing to you, then get out of the business NOW because there are plenty of other mediocre LO's in every city in this country...consumers deserve better. OR, decide today is the day I will start studying what unicorns do and then *get busy taking action immediately.*

BEHAVIOR OF PASTURE GRAZING HORSE LO'S:

- Asking agents to send a referral
- Hey, how about we grab lunch or a coffee (via text or email)

- Sending marketing items of a package via snail mail as an introduction.

- Creating open house flyers for the Realtor to take.

- Having set hours or parameters around times that you're available.

- Acting like someone owes you something because of some past performance.

- Sitting next to the phone, keyboard, deal, or bar waiting for that next opportunity.

THE BEHAVIOR OF UNICORNS LO'S:

- Hold both consumer & agent open houses with (not send them some flyer to use) either that current unicorn LO or soon-to-be. You won't find any other LOs out doing this, and if by some chance you do, give them a high five and start to develop a working relationship with them because they're going places.

- Stop offering to pay for things (you're not supposed to anyway). Here is a new one: commit to the Realtor partners you're targeting so that no one will outwork, out-hustle, or out-commit to their clients more than you. Doing this will help the Realtors make more than either could comprehend.

- When the Realtor gives you a shot, you better turn it into an extra-base hit because if you're striking out and taking walks early in the game, doubt sinks in, and you look the the same as all the others.

- Stop talking about programs, and rates, but do speak of service and belief and passion regarding your why and purpose. Make them feel inspired about how you walk and talk

Two final thoughts to meld your mind around...look around for one of these unicorn v unicorn matchups in the Realtor/Loan Officer realm. Please don't ask them to break their bond and all the reasons why you're better...Stop that! This is slimy, cheesy & distasteful behavior. Ask them why their commitment and bond are so strong, study them, and then go out and form you're own because, after all, once you create the U v U relationship with a Realtor, don't you desire that they take themselves off of the open market and commit to a business partnership with you vs. always falling victim to the, "I have a buyer referral for you" because we all know what comes after that.

Relationships matter & be the 1st to do the good deed without any expectation of reciprocity and treat everyone well, if for no other reason than how you treat people will seriously impact you're outcome and longevity.

I hope this chapter has reinvigorated you to attend Unicorn Bootcamp and start scouting for your Unicorn because you can launch or relaunch momentum with just one.

Your potential is limitless. With consistent, disciplined action, you'll realize you can break through boundaries you've allowed this world and others to set for you.

Make a difference, change one life today, and this approach may just change yours too.

MARK PERKINS

The Power of Personal BRANDING

Presented by:

 Survey Loop

In the ever-evolving lending landscape - the Next Gen Loan Officer occupies a unique position - a position where the power of personal branding and digital presence reign supreme.

Consider the pivotal role of social media in shaping the homebuying journey of today's consumers. Platforms like TikTok, YouTube, and Instagram have become the go-to sources for financial education and advice, especially for millennials and Gen Zers. Within this digital world, Loan Officers can wield significant influence as "finfluencers", guiding aspiring homeowners through the intricacies of the buying process.

But being a Next Gen Loan Officer transcends the traditional notions of age - it's about embracing a forward-thinking mindset and leveraging digital tools to connect with clients in meaningful ways. This section and the chapters in it explore the profound impact of social platforms on the lending industry and the immense potential they offer for personal branding and client engagement.

Through the lens of personal branding, this section of the book will dive into strategies for harnessing the power of social media to establish credibility, build trust, and ultimately, drive business growth.

From crafting compelling content to cultivating an authentic online presence, Next Gen Loan Officers can elevate their professional brand and stand out in a crowded marketplace.

As you read through the chapters ahead, remember that success in today's lending landscape isn't just about closing deals - it's about building lasting connections and fostering trust through digital engagement. So, are you ready to harness the power of social media and unlock new opportunities? Let's jump in and discover how personal branding can propel you forward as a Next Generation Loan Officer!

CHAPTER 7:
Differentiating Yourself
From Your competition

You are not alone. You are not alone even when you are alone, thanks to social media. However, you are also not alone in feeling alone when it comes to trying to get attention on social media.

A good salesperson never needs to act like one. He was born to sell. He has one superpower and he'll take any opportunity to use it: closing a deal. The very best sales people aren't even all that interested in closing a deal, they're interested in closing lots of deals. The path to closing lots of deals has evolved significantly over the last generation. It used to be the more doors on which you were willing to knock, the more deals you got. It was part persistence and part skill.

Today, access to more households is significantly easier… or at least lowers the shoe budget. Yet, you can get thousands of views every month and only hear from a few people a quarter. Why do you think that is the case? It is because you are competing. But, you may have no idea who your competition is.

If you sold Hoover vacuum cleaners door-to-door in 1980, who do you think your major competitor was? Oreck? Kirby? Other Hoover reps? No. It was Amway, Tupperware, Cutco, roofers, siding companies, and life insurance reps. You see, more than competing against other vacuums, you were competing with the timing of other products getting to their door (and budget) before you.

The mortgage industry is overwhelmingly consumed with competing for one thing: mortgages. No one needs to be sold a mortgage. No one even wants a mortgage. They want a property. The mortgage industry has neglected to realize the single most important thing it's really competing with: time. This is the core difference between a salesperson and a marketer. Selling is an art. It takes great charisma, that je ne sais quoi that everyone else simply does not possess. But, when you decide to compete on social media, you need to think like a marketer, and marketing is a science.

The science of social marketing has two key factors:

Time and Technology.

Naturally, there is only so much time in a day. When it comes to gaining a new contact's confidence, there's no getting out of the time to build trust. When it comes to your existing audience, there's no getting out of the time to retain trust. Take the time to stay top of mind. Post at least 3 days a week to remind people you're still here. It doesn't have to be overly creative. Just keep showing up!

You are competing for people's bandwidth of time and patience to retain things. You can earn trust simply by being consistent. Why? Because there's a lag.

Lag is just another form of time. It is simply the big gap in it. The longer the lag in a product sales cycle, the more you need to show up. Seems counterintuitive doesn't it? Think of mattress sales. If people only replace a mattress every 8 years on average, then the company CANNOT afford to miss the sale because they'll have to wait another 8 years! But, if you just bought your mattress last week, do you want the mattress company to talk about Posturepedic versus Sealey, a storewide sale, and how they'll deliver to your home on the same day? No. You no longer care about a new mattress. That talk is for paid social media, people who are not already following them.

But, if you followed your mattress company on social media and found their content about you, you would care. They could post about how to make your mattress last longer, how to clean it, a showcase of best mattress pads, a give-away for a comforter set, video of the best furniture configuration in a bedroom, how to make your guests feel comfortable in their bed… you get the point. During the lag of the 8 years, they could keep you so engaged, generally about mattresses, that they are top of mind when you want to purchase again.

The average person sees around 10,000 product brands every single day. From the time he uses his Crest toothpaste, to driving his Lexus to a meeting, to all the signage on the roads, to online ads, emails, and social media posts, there is very little bandwidth left for him to retain one more brand. So, how can you be the one to get his attention? Be his resource!

You can be a resource for almost anything. When dealing with someone's home, you are dealing with their whole life. Be a whole person. You can interview an appraiser to ask what she looks for in value, post the increased value of front yard landscaping, share articles on DIY projects that actually pay off, and talk to homeowners about a cash-out refi who hate their house but love their school district. Make it personal.

People who follow you don't want to hear about rates or products. They're probably still in the ones you gave them. You can pay for campaigns on social media, but every person in your network has a network - and THAT'S who you also need to go after. Being referred is your least expensive, most effective, highest conversion of new clients. So, occasionally ask for the referral in your posts. Like your mattress company, odds are slim that you'd go around your neighborhood talking about it. But, if someone mentioned that it's time to get a new mattress, you wouldn't hesitate to refer it. And, that would make a great post.

Still, it's not enough to connect when people are willing to listen, sales needs to connect with consumers HOW they want to listen. This is why social media is so effective. It is the preferred choice for most people today to learn about new products and opportunities.

Getting easy access to information, quick links to apply, receiving thorough responses, and keeping in touch with a regular cadence are all important to today's consumer, and they require effective technology. Using a CRM, automation and AI are the differentiators between waiting on the door-to-door sales guy to get back to the office to read his handwritten messages and staying ahead of the competition by inquiries having no lag in waiting at all.

Time and technology are at the intersection of sales success. Hear this video from Leopard Job to learn more about how to use them to Find Your Spot in mortgage.

"Your videos are a version of you that are out there networking and connecting with others 24/7."

CHAPTER 8:
The Pain Point Pitch

Somehow, at the time of this book's publishing (early 2024) there are still mortgage professionals out there that aren't convinced video content works.

If you're one of the skeptics, scan the QR code. I have a few stats for you.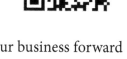

If you're not a skeptic, let's help you drive your business forward with some of the best video content possible, shall we?

Before we dive in, let's make something clear:

video content is NOT "Social Media." video content is a marketing asset.

What is believed to be the oldest surviving video ("motion picture") was made in October of 1888. Video has existed since before any of us were born, and it will exist long after. The thing that changes is how you get your videos in front of people.

Social Media is for connecting, engaging, networking, and being social (it's kind of in the name). Social Media Platforms are also a distribution channel for video content. And this distribution channel is FREE!

Sure, you can run paid ads to your hearts content but, for the first time in history, paying is not a requirement. That's a powerful thing… if you use it to your advantage.

But don't stop with social media. Video content has been proven to increase open rates for email campaigns, improve response rates in text message outreach, give websites an SEO lift when included on key pages, and a whole lot more.

While many of us make video with social media in mind, if you're not repurposing it in other ways, you're not getting the most out of it.

When it comes to creating video content to grow your brand, and your business, it's not as easy as it used to be. Because we all have a capable video camera in our pocket these days, there is a ton of video out there competing for the attention of viewers. Quality matters more every day.

Don't make the mistake of thinking "quality" refers to "production value," though. Fancy cameras and microphones aren't the quick fix many think they are.

Authenticity, relatability, and the quality of your message are the keys.

I know… you hear that all the time. And people are saying it because it's true.

People don't want to do business with businesses.
People want to do business with people.

 Scan the QR code to the left and I'll explain how getting in the right mindset can help you be more authentic and relatable in your content.

And speaking of those people you want to be doing business with... you need to know who they are.

Who is your target viewer?

Is it a first-time homebuyer in their late-20s with a W2 job who can afford a housing payment, but is having trouble coming up with the 20% down that Uncle Ned said they needed?

Maybe it's a top-producing real estate agent in your area who is constantly struggling to find a reliable mortgage professional who will pick up the phone?

You could, and should, have multiple target viewers for your video content. However, each video should only speak to one of them. Who you are speaking to will change the context of your message, which is why no single video is for everyone... because content for everyone resonates with no one.

Getting detailed in your target viewer descriptions will also help you picture exactly who you're talking to once you start recording. This will help you craft a more relatable message and allow you to be more conversational in your delivery.

Every great piece of content begins and ends with the viewer. Don't start recording a video until you know exactly who you're making it for.

Once you know who you're making a video for, you must resist the urge to sell.

Sorry… I need to say it again…

RESIST THE URGE TO SELL!

Creating and publishing video content is marketing… not sales.

Sales is for immediate, short-term results. It's indispensable, and a good salesperson is worth their weight in gold. But sales is for getting the commitment from the customer and closing the deal. If you really think about it, this is probably what you spend the least amount of time doing on a day-to-day basis.

Marketing, specifically though video content, is a mid to long-term strategy. It's more of a conversation starter than a lead generator. Your videos are a version of you that are out there networking and connecting with others 24/7.

If you post a bunch of videos that do nothing more than attempt to sell a product or service, they will fall flat every time. You don't want to be the person standing on the corner with a megaphone, right?

Video isn't a sales strategy... It's a way to provide value and connect with people. And those people don't want to be sold. People want to be educated and/or entertained.

Providing that value will earn you the trust of future customers, recruits, and referral partners before you ever meet them.

But if you MUST talk about a product, try talking about the results the product provides.

You and your product are not the hero of the story… your customer is. This is why it's important to ensure your video content highlights your target viewer, and how their problems can be solved.

I like alliteration, so let's call this the "Pain Point Pitch."

Human beings are wired to run from pain much faster than we run towards pleasure. Using this to our advantage can level up your content quickly. And it works because it's actually in our DNA.

Scan the QR code and I'll lay it out for you.

TL;DR: Know who you're talking to, educate, empathize, entertain, position your customer as the hero, be yourself, be consistent, hit the red button… make more video.

The results will come.

*"Your camera is more
than a recording device;
it's your tool to make a
difference."*

Dana Trajcevski

CHAPTER 9:
Why Video Isn't Just a Choice, It's YOUR Responsibility

Hey there! Ever wondered why, despite all our advancements, schools still aren't teaching the nuts and bolts of financial literacy? It's a head-scratcher, right? Well, here's the good news: as loan officers, you are sitting on a treasure trove of knowledge that the next generation of homebuyers is hungry for. And guess what? You've got the perfect tool to share it: **video**.

But it's not just about those who are actively looking; it's also about reaching the countless individuals who don't even realize they could own a home. Yes, there are tons of people out there paying rent because they believe a mortgage is out of reach. They've been left out of the conversation for too long, and you have the power — and I'd argue, the responsibility — to educate them, to show them the possibilities.

Gone are the days when social media was just for sharing cat memes and vacation pics. Today, it's a powerhouse for education and connection. And with the world's media consumption behaviors shifting dramatically, sticking to old-school methods just won't cut it. If you want to remain relevant and truly make a difference, it's time to embrace the change.

So, why video? Because it's the mechanism for good you've been waiting for. It's your chance to turn the tide on financial ignorance and empower a whole new generation with the knowledge they need. And let's face it, with all the tools you have at your disposal now, there's really no excuse not to.

As loan officers, you are not just financiers; you are educators, guides, and, let's face it, sometimes therapists! Your role is evolving, and with it, your methods must too. Video isn't just another tool in the box; it's the tool. It's how you can break down barriers, demystify the mortgage process, and show that you aren't just about numbers; you are about people.

Creating engaging videos is about more than just sharing information; it's about sparking inspiration. As loan officers, your goal isn't just to explain the nitty-gritty of mortgages but to ignite the dream of homeownership. Picture this: a young couple watching your video suddenly realizes, "Hey, we can actually do this. We can own a home." That's the power of inspiration, and that's your goal.

But what if being in front of the camera feels about as comfortable as a fish on a bicycle? No worries! There's a whole world of talented folks and companies out there who can help bring your vision to life.

They're like the ghostwriters of the video world, helping you craft your message, your way, without you having to be the on-screen star.

These companies specialize in understanding your voice and your message and turning it into engaging video content that resonates with your audience. They can work with animations, infographics, or even hire actors to deliver your message. The point is, you don't have to be a Spielberg or a Scorsese to make an impact. You just need to be clear about what you want to say and find the right partners to help you say it.

So, remember, while it's great to be your own star, it's okay if that's not your path. The key is to get your message out there in the most impactful way possible, whether that's you in front of the camera or working with pros to create something special on your behalf.

Let's talk about where your videos will make the biggest splash. You know how we all have that one friend who's great at storytelling at parties, but kind of a wallflower in book clubs? Your videos are a bit like that—they need to find their scene to shine. And the scene? Well, it's ever-changing.

Take a peek at these numbers from a 2023 study published on datareportal.com: 62.4% of folks aged 16 to 64 are using Instagram to check out brands and products. That's a lot of eyes ready to watch your stories! Facebook's not too far behind at 54.2%, and TikTok at 42.6%.

But those looking for a good laugh or something to keep them entertained are scrolling through TikTok at 79.9%. Instagram and Facebook are still in the game here, but TikTok's where the party's at for fun.

What's this mean for you? You've got to mix it up! Each platform is like a different party, with its own vibe and type of guests. You wouldn't tell a funny story the same way at a chill coffee shop hangout as you would at a lively birthday bash, right? Same goes for your videos. The trick is to tweak them just a bit to fit where they're going. A snappy start might grab those TikTok scrollers, while a thoughtful intro could engage the Facebook crowd who's there for a deeper dive.

But hey, don't get too comfy with just one platform. It's like having a favorite coffee shop that suddenly closes down— you've got to have a backup! Today's hot spot could be tomorrow's ghost town. Spreading your content across different platforms means you're always where the audience is, even if they move on to the next big thing.

Now, I'm not saying you need to create entirely different videos for each place. Who has the time for that? It's about those little tweaks. Imagine you're telling your story in different rooms of the same house. The core of it stays the same; it's just the delivery that changes.

So, remember, it's not just about making great content; it's about making it great for where it's going. Keep an eye on the trends, know your platforms, and be ready to adapt. Your audience is out there, hopping from one scene to the next. Make sure your videos are ready to meet them wherever they are, and you'll be the one setting the trend.

As you're gearing up to step in front of the camera, remember that this journey is as much about connection as it is about education. I've shared insights and tips in my blog posts, but it's also worth noting that this chapter's co-author, Jillian Sorensen, brings an invaluable perspective on making your videos feel genuine and engaging; avoid the teleprompter. In her writings, Jillian emphasizes that while a teleprompter might seem like a safety net, it often saps the life out of your delivery. Your goal is to converse with your audience, not read to them. Instead of a word-for-word script, work with bullet points that outline your message. This approach keeps your delivery natural and allows your true personality to shine through.

When you speak, imagine a friendly face on the other side of the lens. This isn't just about dispensing wisdom; it's about sharing a part of yourself. If you misspeak or lose your train of thought, just pause, smile, and continue. These moments don't detract from your message; they enrich it by showcasing your authenticity.

And remember, practice makes perfect. The more you engage with your audience through the lens, the more natural it will become. Jillian and I encourage you to embrace your unique style and story. Your viewers are there for the real you, the one who laughs, makes mistakes, and most importantly, cares deeply about empowering them with knowledge.

So, take a deep breath, press record, and start the conversation. Your journey to becoming camera-ready is not just about perfecting your delivery, but about opening up a world of possibility for your audience. Together, we're not just teaching; we're inspiring a new generation of homeowners.

We've journeyed through the landscape of social media, the power of video, and the art of connecting authentically with our audience. It's clear that as loan officers in this rapidly changing world, you are no longer just financial advisors; you are educators, storytellers, and catalysts for change. Your mission goes beyond transactions; it's about transforming the dream of homeownership into a tangible reality for everyone.

Remember, every video you post, every story you share, is a chance to demystify the complex world of mortgages, to light up a path to homeownership that many thought was hidden. We're not just sharing information; we're sparking inspiration and building a community of informed, empowered future homeowners.

Now, it's over to you. Your camera is more than a recording device; it's your tool to make a difference. Don't wait for the perfect moment or the perfect video. Start where you are, use what you have, and do what you can. Embrace the bloopers, celebrate the successes, and grow with every click of the record button.

Remember, you don't have to go at it alone. Collaborate with experts, or with co-authors and colleagues who bring their own unique perspectives and insights.

Most importantly, keep your audience at the heart of every video you create. Listen to their needs, understand their fears, and be the guiding light on their journey to homeownership. So, pick up that camera, press record, and step into your role as an educator, an inspirer, and a beacon of hope. The next generation of homeowners is waiting, and the future is bright.

Let's show them the way, one video at a time.

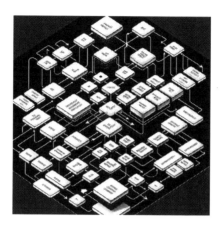

CHAPTER 10:
Personal Brand = Thought Leadership =Sales

Your personal brand is your professional reputation and how your peers, clients, leads, and community perceive you. This is the foundation for Thought Leadership and closing more sales.

Let's be honest, you're probably over the term "Personal Brand" right? It's come up A LOT over the past few years as everyone has tried to crack the code on how to sell more online and leverage social media.

However, those social media experts and the ones crushing it online aren't wrong.

But what IS your personal brand?

The colors, fonts and logo for your website? To me, that is the RESULT of your personal brand in digital form and honestly, these should be the least of your worries.

In this chapter we're going to dive into HOW to identify your personal brand, WHY this needs to get figured out before you do anything else online and its role in helping others see you as a Thought Leader.

I recognize the term, Thought Leader, is severely overused these days so we'll toggle back and forth between 'the go-to person in your industry' and 'expert in your space' here (they all mean the same thing).

Before we go any further, I want you to grasp the significance of this... knowing how to communicate your personal brand, build it online and be seen as the expert in your space is directly tied to you closing more sales.

Let's look at some data to back this (I promise I'm not making this up!) Write these numbers down and remember them as you go throughout this process (or if you ever get stuck pushing 'post' on some content on social media)

$$75$$
$$8$$
$$50$$

75: 75% of buyers say that thought leadership content helps them determine who they want to buy from now or in the future.

8: 8 out of 10 buyers say that thought leadership content helps them determine who they want to learn and educate themselves from.

50: almost 50% of business decision-makers say that thought leadership content is what helps them determine who they want to partner and do business with.

This probably makes sense as you see this laid out before you.

Can you think of someone or some brand that you buy from based on their marketing and branding with this strategy in mind?

They educate and add value to you therefore you trust them more and more, which means you like them, which means you'll do business with them. We want the same thing for you.

So, let's dive into a framework that can help you define your personal brand.

THE 5 C'S FRAMEWORK

The 5 C's of Personal Branding is a concept that can be used to identify the key components of your personal brand. It includes Clarity, Consistency, Character, Connection, and Credibility. By understanding how each of these aspects works together to create your own unique personal brand, you will be able to differentiate yourself from others in the industry, attract more opportunities, connections, and sales all while feeling 100% authentically YOU.

Let's go...

C#1: CLARITY

Clarity refers to having a clear and well-defined personal brand message. It means being able to articulate who you are, what you do, and what makes you unique. When building your online personal brand, it's important to clearly communicate your values, expertise, and the benefits you offer to your audience. Clarity helps you stand out and attract the right audience who resonate with your brand AKA your ideal client.

C#2: CONSISTENCY

Consistency means maintaining a consistent brand image and message across all online platforms and interactions. It involves using the same branding elements such as logo, color scheme, visual style, profile photo on all platforms. More importantly, it also applies to the content you create and share, ensuring that it aligns with your personal brand values, tone, and style. Consistency helps build trust and recognition among your audience.

C#3: CHARACTER

Character refers to the personality of the brand – your personality! It's about how you communicate and engage with your audience, and the emotional response you evoke in others. Your character can be defined as professional, friendly, innovative, traditional, etc., depending on your values and target audience.

**My advice: when you're creating content, write just like you talk. When you're chatting with someone over messenger, type as though you're having an in-person conversation. Those aspects of you make up your unique brand.

c#4: CONNECTION

Building a connection with the audience is key and honestly, it's the thing that makes you human in a digital space. This means you're creating an emotional bond with your audience and customers, speaking to their needs and preferences, and engaging with them in a meaningful way.

c#5: CREDIBILITY

Credibility is about earning the trust of the audience. It's achieved through demonstrating your expertise and creating valuable content, keeping them up to speed with what's going on in the market and in your industry, sharing client testimonials, reviews, and case studies, being honest and transparent, and engaging regularly with your audience.

By walking through this framework, not only will you become more aware of how you want to present yourself to your audience and customers, but you create and identify a personal brand with intention and authenticity.

The next part is now making your audience and ideal customers AWARE of your personal brand so that they see you as the go-to expert.

This part is really up to you and knowing your ideal client best. Where do they hang out online? Which platform do you want to connect with them on?

In my opinion, LinkedIn is one of THE best places you can spend your time creating content and connecting directly with folks who would love to work with you. Not only is it the best place to find professionals to work and connect with in any industry, but it's a place where people SEEK OUT industry leaders.

The audience there is looking for YOU, yes loan officers, real estate agents, brokers, lenders, etc. they're all there. AND so are home buyers. WIN WIN.

BUT this chapter isn't about LinkedIn, it's about helping you identify your personal brand so you can maximize it on the platform of your choosing – but I still would really love to see you leverage LinkedIn!

If LinkedIn is something you need more help with and want to learn more, I gotchu. Scan the QR code below to see how simple LinkedIn can be to build an audience, grow your reach and be seen as the go-to expert in order to help, serve and sell more.

CHAPTER 11:
The Do's & Don'ts of Personal Branding

I have coached a lot of professionals on how to develop a personal brand. Coming in to our conversation, many mistakenly think that brand has everything to do with the perfect logo or a clever name and tagline. Those topics are components of the discussion to be sure, but it's not where the conversation starts.

Just like in the mortgage industry, Marketing uses a lot of terms interchangeably. It's very important that you understand how you're using the words and whether you're describing an idea, an activity, a process, or a tangible element. Let's clear this up...

Brand:
Someone's experience or perception of engaging with you or your service.

Branding:
The process of actively shaping the perception, reputation, and public opinion of a brand.

Brand Identity:
The tangible, visual, or audible representations of a brand (logo, tag line, jingle, headshot, color palate, website, and even tone of voice in your communications)

The simplest definition of brand is *"someone's experience in working with you."* This is not an oversimplification. It's a spot-on definition. Yet so many people overcomplicate it with discussions of logos, vanity URLs, and tag lines.

Here's an example of what this definition means… If I say to you the word "Nike," what immediately comes to mind?

Given a few seconds to ponder, you'd probably mention their iconic swoosh logo, the pair of Jordans you have in the closet, or legendary commercials with prominent athletes in their prime.

But that's not the same thing as me asking, "What is your experience in consuming Nike products?"

Your answer to that question is not going to be, "Swoosh!" You're going to describe the impression you have for their products based on your experience as a consumer: good, bad, or indifferent. THAT is Nike's brand… to YOU. Because every time you see that iconic logo, those feelings (good, bad, or indifferent) are going to be what come to mind.

Did you know that the Nike logo was designed for a total of $35 by designer Carolyn Davidson? It's had a few touch-ups along the way, but the design you see today is pretty close to the original concept.

Conversely, British Petrol (BP) paid a whopping $210 Billion (yes, billion) in the mid-2000s for their iconic green lettering and floral-infused logo to showcase their company's environmental focus. Chalk one up for irony, right?

What stands out to you when you see the BP logo? Their decades of work for environmental advocacy or the worst catastrophe to strike the Gulf of Mexico?

At least Davidson later received 500 shares of Nike stock for her efforts. A logo means nothing if what it stands for is out of alignment with reality.

It takes time and effort to build a personal brand. The kind of time and effort that very few people are willing to invest. Yet coming up with the cutesy name and the crappy logo they got for $20 on Fiverr is where the vast majority will start instead of putting a heavy dose of thinking into the process to develop that brand the right way.

Here are my tips on the most important "Do's & Don't's" when it comes to building a personal brand.

THE DO'S:

Think about what kind of professional you want to be.

Visualize what that person looks like. If that future professional doesn't match who you are today in terms of habits, mindset, and work ethic; then you have other things to focus on first.

Make room for your brand to evolve.

The foundational principles won't change, but how it looks to your future audience will. Give yourself the grace and flexibility to adapt and grow.

Do a URL search of your FirstAndLastName.com.

You 100% control your name, so leverage it. If it's available, grab it IMMEDIATELY. Your name is synonymous with your brand and it is one of the easiest (and safest) ways to market yourself in the future.

Google is your best friend!

If you're ready to start branding around a concept, Google it. This is an easy way to see if there's anyone else using the same name (especially in your market) and how successful they are at promoting it. It gives you a clear picture of the road ahead.

Talk to someone proficient at Marketing & Branding!

The more you engage one-on-one with someone possessing extensive branding experience, the better the questions tend to be. Consider finding an expert outside of the mortgage and real estate industry to advise you. It's worth the investment of both money and time if you plan to have a lengthy and successful career.

THE DON'TS:

Don't waste time trying to come up with a clever name.

The hardest conversations I have are with the folks who have already decided "this or that" name is what they want. Because I first have to undo all the wrong thinking that went into it for us to have a constructive conversation about what will work for them.

Don't succumb to FOMO, emotions, or ego as a motivator for the brand you develop.

These factors are a bit more subtle and harder for someone to admit to themselves. But others can see it. Your community will see it. And they will choose not to engage with you if those factors are the foundation for your brand.

Don't spend thousands of dollars with a broker to secure a URL that's already taken based on that clever name.

I've seen people spend in the four and five figures to secure a URL based on a brand idea that I knew was not going to work for them.

Do not think a branding move will suddenly transform your business.

This is a process that takes time. It's the long-term play in a very transitory industry and it's going to take a long-term commitment on your part.

Do not ask your social media community for advice!

Your Facebook friends are not the right focus group. Most will say, "Yeah, it's great!" because they want to be supportive. It becomes an echo chamber reinforcing a bad idea.

BONUS PRO TIP:

In the absence of branding that you have 100% confidence building your career around, you don't need a personal logo (or even a team logo). Your company's logo will work just fine. If you disagree, or if that is not an attractive solution for you, then the question you need to answer is,

"Why are you with that company?"

Social Media is HERE TO STAY

Presented by:

We hope you are ready to go deep into the indispensable influence of social media on the mortgage industry's future.

Starting with a Gen-Z's perspective on bridging the generational gap, the narrative evolves through strategic insights on employing social media, podcasting, and effective personal branding to redefine industry standards. This section not only affirms the enduring presence of social media but also showcases its critical role in connecting with the next generation of borrowers, establishing industry authority, and nurturing meaningful relationships. Through a blend of personal anecdotes, proven strategies, and the innovative WIN Framework, it provides loan officers with a dynamic playbook to excel in a digital-centric market, ensuring they remain at the forefront of innovation and customer engagement in the rapidly evolving landscape of real estate finance.

"It's a whole new world in mortgage. Grab your oxygen and enjoy the journey."

Greg Sher

CHAPTER 12:
Is Social A Real Strategy

It was late November 2020 when it hit me. That was my moment of epiphany, the moment I knew the mortgage business would never be the same again. It had nothing to do with Covid, although the pandemic accelerated the adoption of social media in mortgage with so many folks locked up at home looking for something to do. It was then that I started following a real-life trailblazer by the name of Scott Betley, although you may know him on tiktok and Instagram as "thatmortgageguy."

Not only was he the most followed licensed originator on tiktok, (he remains #1 today by several hundred thousand), some of his mortgage-related videos would get well over 1 million views.

In nearly all of them, he was wearing his company gear, and his direct messages (DM's) were exploding with questions from interested homebuyers.

I knew right then I was looking at the future.

I immediately reached out to Scott and introduced myself. I said, "I'm sure your current lender is jumping through hoops to embrace and build on this traction you have on social media, but just in case they're not, you are the future." He paused..... those 3-5 seconds felt like an hour. He finally responded; "Actually, they look at me like I'm an alien who just landed on Earth. I get no support. We don't even have a CRM to handle the hundreds of leads some of my videos drive in on a weekly basis. In fact, they recently recognized their top 10 marketers within the company, and I wasn't even on the list."
That was music to my ears.

His company, was like the majority of lenders, both then and now; unequipped and unwilling to embrace a strategy beyond open house flyers and traditional marketing.

Just a few short months later, in April 2021, Scott joined me at NFM Lending and we launched the first-ever "Influencer Division" in the mortgage space.

It has been 32 months since we brought this idea to life and boy, has it come to life!

65,372.

That's how many consumers have raised their hands and asked for more information from NFM, all resulting from videos they watched from our team, a team that now consists of 14 mortgage influencers.

** *For clarification purposes, these are all licensed LO's that work for NFM Lending. They are not paid influencers. They are commissioned LO's.*

Another question often asked is "How much did you spend to bring in those 65,372 consumers?" Zero. Every hand that has been raised came organically, mostly through Tiktok, Instagram, Facebook and Youtube content.

Most telling is the data behind those raised hands:

97% (65,372)   indicated they were interested in purchasing a home

84.5% (53,582)   indicated they did not have an agent yet Of those 84.5%,

94% (50,367)   said they'd welcome an agent introduction

As a whole, the activity of the Influencer Division has led to 1272 closings for $405M in volume since inception, mind you, in the most violent rate environment most of us have ever seen.

The elusive Holy Grail for originators has always been finding a way to get to the consumer before the realtor. As you can surmise from the data, the Holy Grail is right before us.

There are two key components to getting in on this opportunity, an opportunity I believe is in the very early stages (so plenty of time):

✳ Roadmap to getting started

✳ Ensuring you/your lender is equipped to handle a "different kind" of consumer.

TOP 10 WAYS TO GET YOURS:

1 Jump right in—make videos—at least 2 per day, 5 days a week

2 Don't give a shit how you look, sound or how many people view them—just do it

3 Forget about fancy equipment at first use your phone

4 Start by talking about an area where you feel you're a subject matter expert

5 Spread your content out across the four major social platforms, Tiktok, IG, FB and YT

6 Do your research on how to follow trending materials

7 Come to terms with the likelihood that your first 100 videos will feel like a total failure

8 Push through the wall—DO NOT STOP

9 Time block so you have no excuses—can't be halfway in, need to be all-in

10 Follow and like others in the industry. Everyone loves affirmation. You will too. Let them know you're watching (including RE agents)

YOU'RE ONLY HALFWAY THERE:

Nobody said this would be easy.

Now that you're mentally there and ready to roll, be prepared for success. Before you can measure that success by closings and deepening relationships with realtor partners, your success in this new endeavor will hinge on you and your organization's ability to respond to consumers in seconds, even if you're not licensed in the state they're inquiring about. Say what? Yup. That's right. I said it. You just committed to building a brand. Now you *need to protect* it.

#1 Make sure you have a strategy to respond to every DM, every inquiry, and every lead form that's filled out.

#2 Have your marketing team create a landing page and place a link to it under your social profiles so consumers can inquire. Linktree is also an option if your lender isn't prepared to assist here.

#3 Have your marketing team set up workflows to ensure optimal automation based on the consumer's answers (example may be the consumer indicated their credit is sub-580, automation would push them into an education platform like Finlocker so they can be nurtured until ready).

#4 Best as an originator to dive into this with a lender that's licensed nationally so you can help more of your followers and YOU can get paid, even when they close in a state you're not licensed in (referral fee).

#5 For this to really work, it must work for your lender too. Make sure you're aligned with a company that sees what you see and that shares the vision that this is an investment worth making in you and the future. It's impossible for your lender to get a preview of every video you create. That is a non-starter. Just get the rules from them and don't break them. There has got to be a level of trust there or your DOA. You likely already know how prepared your lender is to tackle this head-on. If the marketing department is still focusing on flyers and business cards, it's unlikely you're with a lender that's going to "get it" anytime soon.

#6   Because you're getting to the consumer much earlier in the lead funnel, be prepared for some transactions not to take place for as long as a year or two. Some will happen much faster for sure, but most will take some hand-holding, patience, and a lot of education from you to prepare them for their big purchase. This is why having your lead systems and touch points will be essential.

If you're not convinced this is where your business needs to go yet, consider a study conducted by Rocket Mortgage in July 2023 that suggests roughly 45.8% of Gen Z's hope to purchase a home in the next 2-3 years. That's 31M of them.

For context, Gen Z's peak age will be 27 at the time of print. Most germane to this topic is the fact they are the first generation of digital natives to enter the housing market. They spend 3 hours every single day on their mobile phones and much of their buying behavior is conditioned by those they follow with influence.

A survey conducted by Property Trade Magazine in April 2023, revealed that 84% of first-time buyers utilized social media for guidance, advice, and hacks on homeownership.

There are so many byproducts that come with putting yourself out there. One of the biggest gains will be with realtors in your area. They will take notice. Just making the effort will inspire other loan officers and realtors to ask you "how you did it." This will present opportunities to build your business you otherwise would never have.

It's a whole new world in mortgage.

Grab your oxygen and enjoy the journey.

They are not ready to close yet, which takes *patience.*

CHAPTER 13:
who is Gen Z?

After I graduated from FSU in 2021 (Go Noles!!), I went to work for Oracle and Dell Technologies selling their technology stacks. Coming from two large tech giants and then entering the mortgage industry as a twenty-three-year-old, I quickly concluded that the real estate finance world has a lot of innovating to do in order to keep up with the world around us and better serve my generation.

My goal throughout this chapter is to help you, the reader, better understand just who Gen-Z is and how we as an industry can educate and help that next-generation borrower be successful.

I will never forget attending my first mortgage conference with the ActiveComply team during the Summer of 2022. It was a challenging time for our industry and the energy in the conference room was rather stressful.

However, one of the optimistic sessions I attended was about *"Understanding Gen-Z Borrowers"*. It was a roundtable discussion on the characteristics of Generation Z and how to help them achieve homeownership. As I scanned the room of mortgage professionals and listened to the conversations, I realized that while most contributors were discussing their children, siblings, next-door neighbors, etc., I was the only true Gen-Z individual in the room. Once I left that conference, I had a refreshing outlook on the mortgage world. I thought, *"Here is an industry full of very experienced individuals (that is the nice way to put over 40)... And how cool is it that they are wanting to better understand and serve my generation".*

For the months following that conference season, I decided to set out on a goal to *"bridge the gap"* between the mortgage industry and the men & women in my age group. I went on to survey the Gen-Z men and women in my life through a series of survey questions about homeownership and communication styles. From there I started to conduct one-on-one interviews with Gen-Z'ers who had either recently bought a home or stated they were interested in buying a home. I thought it would be insightful to share some powerful quotes that may help you understand my generation better.

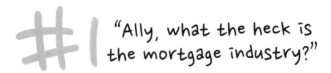

1 "Ally, what the heck is the mortgage industry?"

Contrary to popular belief, my generation was not as impacted by the 2008 financial crisis as much as previous generations. While most industry executives may assume that Gen-Z has a negative outlook on the mortgage world (much like their millennial predecessors) – it turns out they have NO OUTLOOK ON THE MORTGAGE INDUSTRY... Which actually might be worse.

When I first moved to Nashville and I was making new friends, we'd typically ask each other about our occupations. Every time I would say, "I work in the mortgage industry", most of my friends would respond with "ok and what is the mortgage industry".

There is not enough talk about career paths within mortgage and therefore not many young professionals are even aware of the opportunities for a job in our industry. This means there is also a lack of conversation about what it means to own a home and the financial journey in homeownership.

TIP
Remind your network and your group of friends what you do for a living.

The easiest way to do this is to pull some professional content into your personal social media – even if it is just a story on your Instagram or Facebook account about what's going on in the mortgage industry today. This will most likely cause your viewers/followers to think "Oh yeah!! I totally forgot he/she did mortgages", and if they know anyone needed to talk about financing a home they are more likely to remember that is your expertise.

For example, one of my interviewees stated that he found his LO on Instagram. They had gone to college together but had not reconnected in a few years. He said, "All of a sudden she was posting about loans and I messaged her and asked if that was what she was doing now". It's crazy how a simple post like this can create opportunities with people already in your network.

If social media isn't your forte (maybe this book will encourage you to rethink this), it is still a great practice to message or reach out to your friends and ask if they know anyone looking to buy a home. If you're curious if Gen-Z men & women in your life would be annoyed by this question – I do not believe so. My conversations showed that a lot of Gen-Z is eager to help those they trust and a simple ask for a referral is definitely not frowned upon

#2 "well I just thought I needed $100,000 saved before talking to a realtor about buying a home"

Haha – this is probably my favorite quote ever.

Not only was this interviewee misinformed when it comes to a down payment, but it seems that "affordable down-payment options" is the message that our industry is desperately trying to get across to that next-generation borrower. The second part of this quote that I find so interesting is the fact that her first thought was to turn to a realtor versus a loan officer.

TIP

Whether you are a Gen-Z yourself or you are trying to reach my generation, it is no secret that the financial roadmap in buying a home is not discussed enough at an early age. Most people think buying a home is so incomprehensible that they decide to not even look into it.

I'd advise LOs (to again) lean in on their social media strategy to educate – it is free and can reach a large amount of potential prospects at once. Talk about down payment (ensure all compliance measures are in place if you're giving specific examples of financial situations), and talk about the realistic down payment examples for first-time homebuyers. This will help your Gen-Z audience really get their gears turning once they realize the actual numbers.

Realtors do an amazing job of meeting their ideal audience where they are today. A good way to overcome the realtor > loan officer ideology is to ROMATICIZE YOUR JOB!! If you are happy and you have a great "why" in the industry, share that with your friends and across your social media network. Once we as an industry start being a point of conversation alongside the realtors – the borrowers will most likely realize the importance of having a financial plan before reaching out to a realtor.

 **"I found out about an FHA loan from TikTok"**

While most Gen-Z stereotypes may be a bit overexaggerated (like calling all Gen-Z lazy), the stereotype that we "practically live on social media" is not overexaggerated. Statistics show that my generation spends about four hours a day on social media. I just checked my screen time for today and it was 3 hours and 49 minutes (4:30 pm), and I can guarantee you most of it was spent scrolling TikTok and Instagram. .

While 10 years ago Facebook was the primary social media for individuals at the home-buying age, today Instagram and even TikTok prove to be the go-to platforms for that age range.

TIP
Figure out who you want to reach, and meet them there!

When I sent out a survey to my group of individuals aged between 19 – 29, I asked "Which social media platform do you use the most?"

32% TikTok
68% Instagram
0% Twitter
0% Facebook

If your target audience is 50 years and older, maybe start really pushing social media across Facebook. If your target audience is the Gen-Z age group – you will find success primarily on Instagram, TikTok & YouTube.

Now I say "success" with a grain of salt, because my definition of success across social media is not based on likes, comments, or views. My idea of success is based on posting content the creator is passionate about and they are posting content consistently. The likes and views will come, but it is really easy for Gen-Z to see a lack of genuineness when LOs are posting just because they feel like they have to. Believe in what you're educating/posting about and the traction will soon follow.

At the end of the day – Gen-Z is essentially what we all as a population have slowly evolved into. We all rely on the convenience of digital technology, we all lean on referrals from friends whether that be via social media or the local neighborhood gossip, and we all have a dream of owning our own home.

It is our duty as mortgage professionals to meet that next-generation borrower where they are today. Together, we can hopefully change the narrative of homeownership from un-obtainable to "Rolling Out the Welcome Mat".

Gen Z Trends:

"Authenticity Is Key: Be yourself. Your listeners can sense authenticity, and it's what will keep them coming back for more."

Dustin Owen

CHAPTER 14:
Unleashing the Power of Podcasting

In the ever-evolving landscape of sales and marketing, one medium has risen to the forefront, captivating audiences and establishing a unique connection between hosts and listeners – podcasting. As a sales professional, you may wonder how a podcast can be a game-changer for your career. In this chapter, I'll explore the essence of podcasting, its origins, and how you can harness its power to become a local authority, attract ideal clients, and elevate your personal brand.

PODCASTING 101:
Talk Radio Reinvented

At its core, a podcast is akin to a talk radio show on-demand. Listeners can access episodes whenever and wherever, transforming mundane commutes or workout sessions into valuable learning experiences. The beauty of podcasting lies in its accessibility – all you need is a smartphone, an internet connection, and a desire to engage with compelling content.

The origins of podcasting can be traced back to the early 2000s, with pioneers like Dave Winer and Adam Curry leading the way. The term "podcasting" itself is a mashup of "iPod" and "broadcasting," reflecting its roots in making audio content available to a broader audience. What began as a niche hobby soon blossomed into a global phenomenon, with millions of podcasts covering an array of topics.

Fast forward to today, and podcasts have become an integral part of our media landscape, with everyone from celebrities to industry experts leveraging this platform to share insights, stories, and expertise.

THE LOCAL ADVANTAGE:
You Don't Have to Go National

I am Dustin Owen. I am the creator and host of The Loan Officer Podcast, a nationally recognized show. However, the power of podcasting lies not just in its national reach but in its ability to connect on a local level. You don't need a nationwide audience to reap the benefits; instead, your goal is to position yourself as the go-to expert in your local community.

In fact, you don't even need to have a crazy following of tens of thousands of downloads to make your podcast a "success".

Your podcast becomes a vehicle to establish authority, build relationships, and attract ideal clients right in your backyard. Think of it as a personalized, virtual handshake with your community – a way to introduce yourself, share your knowledge, and foster a connection that goes beyond the transactional nature of sales.

PODCASTING GOALS:
A Blueprint for Success

Before hitting the record button, it's crucial to define your podcasting goals. As a sales professional, your objectives might include:

Local Expertise:
Position yourself as the go-to authority in your community.

Ideal Client Attraction:
Tailor your content to resonate with your target audience.

Content Repurposing:
Create content that can be repurposed across social media platforms.

Personal Branding:
Elevate your personal brand by being recognized as a podcast host.

With these goals in mind, you're ready to embark on your podcasting journey.

TIPS FOR PODCASTING SUCCESS:
Lessons from The Loan Officer Podcast

Authenticity Is Key: Be yourself. Your listeners can sense authenticity, and it's what will keep them coming back for more. Let your personality shine through, and don't be afraid to share your experiences.

Know Your Audience: *T*o speak effectively to your audience, you must first know them. Define your ideal client and tailor your content to address their needs, challenges, and aspirations.

Educate and Entertain: Balance is key. Your podcast should be a blend of education and entertainment. Inform your audience with valuable insights, but do so in a way that keeps them engaged and entertained.

Quality Matters: While content is king, production quality matters. Invest in a good microphone, create a clean and professional sound, and pay attention to details like music and editing. A polished podcast reflects positively on your brand.

By incorporating these tips into your podcasting strategy, you'll not only connect with your audience but also position yourself as a knowledgeable and approachable authority in your field.

In conclusion, podcasting is not just a trend; it's a powerful tool that can transform your sales career. Whether you aspire to be a local expert, attract your ideal clients, or elevate your personal brand, podcasting offers a unique platform to achieve these goals. So, grab your microphone, hit record, and let your voice be the next resonant note in the symphony of podcasting success.

CHAPTER 15:
Hey! You're the LinkedIn girl!

If you're in sales, it's essential for people to know what you do. One night I was out with friends when a stranger walked up to me and loudly said "Hey! You're the LinkedIn girl! I love your mortgage posts! If I ever need a home loan, I sure know who to call!" Shortly before this encounter, I questioned if the energy I was putting into social was worth it. Local lenders were barely using the platform (back in 2016) and I wondered if social would fizzle out. It hit me that night with friends that I was reaching people with my posts, and I didn't even realize it! It also was for no cost! The gentleman who approached me that evening knew who I was and that I was a lender in his city. I wondered how many more people could be reached if I was even more intentional with my engagement and content.

content creates conversations. conversations create trust. Trust creates relationships.

We know trust and relationships are essential in the mortgage industry. You need trust for referral partners to recommend their buyers to you, and you need trust for potential clients to become lifelong ones. Now more than ever you have this remarkable ability to create authentic relationships and drive substantial business with potential customers and referral networks…by creating trust virtually!

Let's discuss a common scenario we lenders experience and why your online presence is crucial. A realtor recommends multiple mortgage originators to their new homebuyer and tells them to "shop around".

As you know, most lenders have similar products and rates, and some may do excellent work just like you. Today's buyer likely isn't walking into your office for a meeting like they once did. They're relying on the internet to tell them about you. How are you standing out as credible and trustworthy as they hit the search button with your name? How many Google reviews do they see? Are they witnessing you being interviewed on podcasts as the mortgage expert? Are your videos popping up educating consumers on buying a home? Do they see posts of you volunteering at the animal shelter or coaching your son's soccer game? Homebuyers want to know who is handling their enormous and often emotional financial purchase. They're intelligent and are taking time to research lenders both professionally and personally. Online is the first place they will start their hunt for a dependable loan officer.

TRY THIS ACTIVITY.

Google the words 'loan officer' and the city and state you're in. Do you show up at the top of lenders with reviews or perhaps not at all? Now search your full name. What is appearing? Remember, potential customers are seeing what you're seeing! On an initial call or email intro, I share with my clients a QR code that sends them to all my social media accounts and Google reviews. I explain that I get to know incredible details about them in our discovery meeting, and it's just as important they get to know the girl handling one of their largest financial decisions.

The ability to reach masses and establish more relationships is right at our fingertips, yet many loan officers still reject the thought of using social. Some hope it just goes away, but this instrument is continuing to flourish at a rapid pace. Social media is not meant to replace in-person meetings or events, but it's an additional arrow in your quiver for substantial business evolution! So, why are masses of sales professionals choosing not to use these tools if they know they're extraordinarily effective?

Even when we see the opportunities social has, many are stuck with that dread of posting due to fear. "What will strangers say? Who will judge my makeup? What will my colleagues think about my post about getting pre-qualified? What if I share my opinion only to have others come trolling in?" Trust me. I get it! I felt the same way when I first started posting and even feel it today. If fear tries to sneak in, I remember a quote I heard that has stuck with me. "My imperfect post is better than the post I never did." By consistently showing up online and even having bloopers or errors in your videos as you speak, it reminds your audience you're human and gives the feeling of authenticity. Do you know what attracts other humans? Relatability and imperfection do because ALL humans are imperfect. Don't let paralysis by analysis set in and don't overthink the post.

I also see individuals hitting pause on social because they're underestimating the ability the tool has (just like I did back in 2016). I hear comments like, "I only have 100 followers on Instagram" or "Only ten people liked my post". You must remove this thought process of 'only so many' and think of social from a different viewpoint:

5 followers = a lunch with a real estate brokerage in town

10 likes = a coffee shop of potential new buyers

100 followers = a networking event full of referral partners

500 views = a conference intertwined with connections you could collaborate with

Do 100 followers feel small when you see you can reach the same quantity of people virtually?

I'm going to share a powerful option of utilizing social from a different angle that we often don't hear about. We get caught up in content creation that we forget about ENGAGEMENT. Remember the "content creates conversations" comment? Here's my secret. It's not just your content that creates conversations, it's other's content that allows conversations to happen as well! Social media is supposed to be social! Are you using your platforms to engage, or are you quietly scrolling by other's posts and occasionally liking them? Do you ever have someone comment on your post or even share it? It's a rush of gratitude! You remember comments and shares because likes get lost.

You might find yourself reciprocating to those who have given you virtual support by sharing and commenting on their content too. There are many ways you can develop deeper online connections. Here are a few engagement ideas:

- Direct message someone who created a post that inspired you.

- Share a connection's educational reel and give them a shout out to your audience.

- Send a podcast to someone and explain why you feel they'd enjoy it.

- Comment with thoughtful words or ask questions about a recent trip someone shared online.

- Send a video message to a connection when it's their birthday instead of writing a typical birthday message on their Facebook wall.

Set aside fifteen minutes at the beginning of each day to intentionally engage with others using some of the ideas above. I enjoy doing this in the morning while sipping my first cup of coffee snuggling my pups before my day takes off. Whether it be multiple platforms or just one, take notice of others. It can be with local professionals, past classmates or even someone you'd love to know better or look up to.

Find meaningful words to genuinely cheer people on virtually. You'll be amazed at what happens when you begin taking interest in others! You never know if a new relationship will form or if you'll secure your biggest client or referral source! Social media has helped break boundaries due to geography and permits us to literally connect with anyone on earth in ways we could only do previously in person.

There is a theory called "Six Degrees of Separation" that any two people in the world are only six or less connections apart. You may have heard of the game around this theory called "Six Degrees of Kevin Bacon" where you take anyone in Hollywood and connect them to Kevin via their roles in six film titles or less. Where am I going with this and how does it relate to social media? Scan the QR code to find out!

I can't wait for you to begin using the "Six Degrees" method as you intentionally lean into social media engagement and start seeing the dots connecting! You could be just one comment or direct message away from seeing a ripple effect of opportunities start pouring into your business.

CHAPTER 16:
The WIN Framework

"If people like you they will listen to you, but if they trust you, they'll do business with you."

~~Zig Ziglar~~ -Dan Smokoska

In this chapter, I'm going to show you how to build a powerful personal brand on social media. I'll do this by introducing you to my WIN Framework: A simple, but effective, brand-building strategy I've developed to help loan officers win more business, land more agents, and never have a cold lead again.

Let's get started!

"If people like you they will listen to you, but if they trust you, they'll do business with you."

Zig Ziglar

THE WIN FRAMEWORK:
Your Secret Weapon to Building a Strong Personal Brand onSocial Media

You can go from "no brand" to "money-making brand" in less than 15 minutes a day.

Let me introduce you to the only brand-building framework you'll ever need: The WIN Framework. It includes three equally important actions you can take every day to build a personal brand on social media that will make people practically beg to do business with.

The WIN Framework:

Write valuable content
Invest the time
Network like hell

Do these three things consistently, and those cold leads you once knew will be gone forever. Let me show you how.

Part #1:
Write Valuable Content

"ABC. Always Be Creating.."

~~-Samwise Didier~~ -Dan Smokoska

There's a psychological principle called the familiarity bias. It basically says the more someone sees you, the more they trust you. So, the goal when building a personal brand is to tap into this bias and to be seen a lot (i.e. to become familiar). And you do this best by creating valuable content consistently. But to do this, it's going to take a mindset shift.

The overwhelming majority of people on social media are what I like to call "scrollers." A scroller is someone who consumes other peoples' content, but never creates their own content – they just keep scrolling. To be clear, this isn't a bad thing. However, for our purposes, scrolling doesn't get us the results we're looking for. And what we're looking for is a powerful personal brand that brings in business.

So, to bring in that business, you'll have to shift your mindset: To one that makes you stop scrolling, and start creating.

Here's an example of how I would answer these questions if my ideal customer was a first-time home buyer:

- ***What are their pain points:*** Down payment concerns, mortgage terminology, unfamiliar with the mortgage process, don't know where to begin, thinking they can't afford a home, a lack of knowledge, getting the best interest rate, etc.

- *What knowledge do I have that my ideal customer is missing:* An understanding of the mortgage process, mortgage products, interest rates, down payment requirements, mortgage terminology, application and approval process, closing process and costs, credit score requirements, etc.

- *How can I help solve these pain points:* Video content, social media posts, infographics, blog posts, webinars, e-books, downloadable guides, podcasts, checklists, email newsletter, live Q&A sessions, client success stories, etc.

Here's why this exercise is so powerful: It provides clarity into knowing who your audience is and what's important to them. And it gives you a ton of valuable content ideas. It's a win-win.

PRO TIPS TO CLOSE THIS OUT:
- know your audience
- Solve their problems
- Don't sell (seriously)

Congrats on nailing down a content strategy! But a content plan alone doesn't build a personal brand. You have to be willing to invest the time it takes to see the results you want. In other words, you have to be consistent.

Part #2:

Invest the Time

*"If you want to be successful, you
need consistency and if you don't
have it, you've got no chance.."*

~~-Paul Merson~~ -Dan Smokoska

Here's the cold, hard truth: If you follow the WIN Framework for six months, you'll build an unstoppable personal brand. If you quit before then, you won't.

Let me answer a few questions I typically get at this point regarding where and how to invest your time:

> **Question:**
> *Does it matter which social platform I choose?*
> **Answer:**
> *No. Pick one, and go all-in.*
> **Question:**
> *Does it matter how often I post?*
> **Answer**:
> *Not at first. Focus on starting, then worry about how often you post.*
> **Question:**
> *What if I don't get any likes or comments on my posts?*
> **Answer**:
> *You won't (at first). Keep posting and engaging (more on that in Part #3 coming up), and the likes will come.*

The goal here is simple, **don't make excuses. Just start.**
And once you've started, don't even think about stopping!

Part #3:

Network Like Hell

*"The currency of real networking
is not greed but generosity."*

~~-Keith Ferrazzi~~ -Dan Smokoska

The truth is, networking on social media is the single most important part of the WIN Framework. Most people think that creating content is the most important part, but they'd be wrong! The real magic happens in the comments and DMs. Why? Because that's where the conversations happen. And if you know anything about networking, conversations create connections. Are you ready to become the networker you were always meant to be? Then, let me introduce you to The Point System.

THE POINT SYSTEM

Point Values:
    1 point: Liking someone's post
    2 points: Commenting on someone's post
    3 points: Sharing someone's post
    4 points: Direct messaging someone
    5 points: Jumping on a Zoom call with someone

Your Goal:
    Get 20 points every day. It doesn't matter how you get these points (liking 20 people's posts, direct messaging 5 people, or any combination of these), just hit your goal and never get a zero.

    This process will take you less than 15 minutes a day and your results will be massive.

WRAPPING IT ALL UP

Alright, it's time to close this chapter out. Here's my parting advice: Stop scrolling and start creating, engaging, commenting, liking, and DM'ing. Do this and you'll win on social media. Do it for six months, and have a personal brand that can't be stopped.

And if you have questions along the way, you can always message me at dan@winsocial.com or DM me on social media at @DanSmokoska.

I'm rooting for you.

Top Producer Perspectives

Presented by:

WINDSOR
MORTGAGE

In this section you'll hear from some of the industry's top originators. Here, industry leaders share their journeys of innovation, specialization, and the profound impact of aligning work with purpose and passion

From the pivotal moments that redefine careers to the art of salesmanship rooted in authenticity, each story encapsulates the essence of what it means to thrive in the evolving landscape of mortgage lending. These pages are filled with wisdom on leveraging personal strengths, embracing educational opportunities, and the significance of focusing on a niche to stand out in a competitive field. Let the experiences and lessons shared here inspire you to forge your path, make meaningful connections, and achieve a fulfilling and successful career in mortgage lending.

CHAPTER 17:
Discovering Your Purpose

Welcome to a transformative journey in the life of a loan officer. I want to share with you a different perspective on your career. This isn't just about closing a lot of loans; it's about discovering your purpose, igniting your passion, and earning profits by doing more of what you love. Yes. It is possible to do more of what you love, less of the things you don't and make more money doing so.

I had spent about 25 years in the mortgage industry when I unintentionally overheard a conversation between two of my adult children in another room. My youngest daughter, who is 13 years younger than her next sibling, was engaged in a discussion with her sister. They were comparing their experiences growing up, talking about the nights I came in late and on the phone, or worse, like when I missed them stealing a base at a ball game because I looked down to send a text or take a call. It was a casual conversation to them almost as if they were laughing about it, but, OUCH!

I am grateful for the sting I felt from that conversation. It was exactly what I needed to hear. I was at the burnout stage in my career, so their conversation had me questioning if I had worked long and hard for nothing. Yes, my family enjoyed all the things they had dreamed for. We have taken nice trips, driven nice cars, lived in great homes. But the things that matter most, like being present, I had failed to give them. Honestly, I am still working on being more present. It's a hard habit to break after spending so many years working around the clock, always available to everyone.

My girls' conversation started me on a journey to get clear about what my purpose is. My purpose is not just about working a lot of hours and being successful in the business. I wanted my life to mean more. I wanted a legacy which put me on a path to discover my why – my purpose.

If you find yourself wanting more than just trophies on the shelf and a big bank account, keep reading. I have been sharing this journey with realtors, loan officers and entrepreneurs in masterminds, through coaching, podcasts and 3-day retreats. It is truly something I am passionate about because I have seen how it changes lives.

DISCOVERING YOUR PURPOSE

Reflect on Your Why: Ask yourself why you chose to be a loan officer. Write down your thoughts. Keep asking second and third level questions of yourself to truly discover your why. It is likely a result of an experience you had long ago. And ask yourself what you do that you enjoy most about helping families into homes.

Understanding your 'why' is the cornerstone of your purpose.

Assess Your Impact: Consider the families you've helped and the differences you've made in their lives. This impact is an integral part of your purpose. Think back to the stories of the families you have served. What are your favorites and ask why that is your favorite story. That will help you discover your purpose. But also go back to the story you discovered about yourself when reflecting on your why. It is YOUR story that creates impact but only when you are willing to share it.

Align with Your Values: What are your core values? Integrity, service, growth? Ensure these align with your professional role. Often the feeling of burn out comes from not aligning your values with your professional life. Your values in your professional life should not be different than your values in your personal life. And your purpose should reflect your values.

Once you understand your purpose, you'll gain clarity on whom you want to serve. This understanding transforms how you approach your business. Instead of just selling, you start providing solutions and resources for your ideal clients. When you start sharing the stories of those you served and how you served, you will be given more opportunities to serve.

THE POWER OF WORDS

Once you have clarity on your purpose and the people you wish to serve, the next step is to articulate your purpose through the power of words. Create an affirmation statement that resonates with your purpose. For example, "I am a dedicated loan officer, committed to helping families achieve their dream of homeownership through teaching them the process and sharing my resources." Recite your purpose daily, asking God, the universe, or your higher power to provide opportunities to serve in a purposeful and fulfilling way. This practice not only

143

reaffirms your commitment but also open doors to new possibilities in your business.

IGNITING YOUR PASSION

Pause and Reflect: Question the routine. Ensure that your daily activities align with your purpose and passions. Your routine should bring you energy and give you the power to go through your day with ease and joy. I understand not every day, all day will feel this way but when it doesn't, review the day from the place of observation, not judgement so you can make intentional adjustments if necessary.

Continuous Learning: Never stop learning anything and everything that interests you. Stay curious in life. Share what you learn in conversations, through masterminds or book clubs, podcasts, social media, etc. When you share what you are learning you are building a community and creating connections with others that align with your passions.

Network with Purpose: Connect with groups and organizations that resonate with your purpose. Enjoy the process of networking; it's where passion thrives.

TURNING PURPOSE AND PASSION INTO PROFIT

Set Clear Goals: What does success feel like to you? Define it in your own way and make it measurable.

Refine your Processes: Leverage technology to streamline your workflow. Efficiency leads to more business and, consequently, higher profits.

Build Relationships: Developing lasting relationships with clients, business partners, and others in your community are key. It's about consistency, intentionality, and authenticity.

But most importantly, maintain a deep connection with yourself, family, and friends. Don't be so busy serving others that you leave yourself and those that matter most to being served last.

Market Yourself: Focus on attracting business rather than chasing it. Engage in community involvement that aligns with your purpose, creating a genuine brand presence.

Sales Conversations: Your conversations become easier when you are passionate about who you want to serve, how you want to serve, what makes you unique. At the end of the day, we are salespeople and success are about connections and conversations. They become easier, and you become more successful when you get clear with your purpose.

CHALLENGING YOURSELF TO GROW

- ☐ **30-Day Purpose Challenge:** Begin each day with a reminder of your 'why'. Say it out loud like an affirmation. Write it down in places you will see during the day.

- ☐ **Passion Project:** Initiate a project that excites you and aligns with your passion serving others.

- ☐ **Profit Plan:** Know your numbers and review them daily.

- ☐ **Self-Assessment:** Begin and end each day with intentional reflection and gratitude.

- ☐ **Mindfulness and Self-Care:** Embrace practices that keep you healthy and happy.

- ☐ **Celebrate Small Wins:** Acknowledge and celebrate daily.

CONCLUSION

This journey is about much more than being a loan officer; it's about creating a fulfilling life and business. It's about transformation. Embrace this challenge, rethink what you thought business is supposed to be like, and remember, in the world of mortgages, you're not just closing loans; you're opening doors to new possibilities.

You're creating a life and business you love, knowing your purpose, abundant in passion, and rewarding in profits. Welcome to your new beginning! *Be legendary!*

"Wealthy people aren't wealthy because they have money, they are wealthy because they have advice and information."

Ryan Grant

CHAPTER 18:
Belief In Action

In the dynamic and competitive world of mortgage lending, belief in your product isn't just a part of the job—it's the very essence of it. As a Mortgage Advisor, standing out isn't just about being different—it's about being better in ways that matter. We need to not only understand what makes our offering more valuable than others, but we also need to genuinely believe in the significance of what we're able to do for our clients.

This chapter delves into why belief is so vital and how it can distinguish our services, even when our clients are continually faced with cheaper competitors.

I remember a time in my career when I just simply wasn't proud of what I was doing. I was among the Top 25 Mortgage Professionals in the country, but if you would have asked me what I did for work, I would have shrugged and dismissively told you that I was in the mortgage business. It was a strange place to be, mentally, because you would think that I would be happy and proud of my "success," but there were so many things happening that made me realize that we had to make a change. After starting to lose clients to cheaper priced lenders, seeing my past clients make bad decisions and get into financial trouble and realizing that I was only being praised for selling debt, not enhancing our clients' lives, we made a decision to change everything. My team said "We are no longer going to be a dollar more expensive than the cheapest lender, unless we can quantifiably show our clients how we're going to help them grow their overall generational wealth.

This feeling was both empowering and scary at the same time. Empowering because I was inspired by what we could do and I knew I would be fulfilled to see the lives of my clients change for the better, but scary because the mortgage industry had never tried to be anything more than just debt salesmen. No one was asking us to do anything more than just take applications, give advice, and close loans on time, with good customer service. Because the bar was so low, we had to start solving problems that most people didn't know they had, and we knew it was going to be a massive undertaking.

When we first started, we developed the philosophy that we would be the most valuable team of people, along with our real estate professionals, in every aspect of our client's real estate and financial lives. Not just for the thirty days of the transaction, but for thirty plus years. I kept asking our clients, why do you want to own real estate and almost always, the answer had something to do with building wealth.

My response to them was that "Wealthy people aren't wealthy because they have money, they are wealthy because they have advice and information." From there, we just showed them the road ahead and explained what we were going to do for them, every step of the way.

Belief in our product goes far beyond knowing the features and benefits of the mortgage instrument that we are known to offer —it's about understanding the role we can play in our clients' lives and the commitment that we can make to them. In doing this, we not only solve our clients' problems, but we do the same for everyone around us.

What I've learned over my career is that the road to success is created by solving other people's problems. The best place to start here is to identify the problems of your target audiences.

THE CONSUMER

They typically don't have a plan for their real estate or financial future. They buy homes on emotion or due to circumstance and once they own a home, they are completely on their own to find out how to be a successful homeowner.

REAL ESTATE PROFESSIONALS

They need help to attract and adopt new clients, well in advance of any transaction.

With all of the issues we're seeing around buyers agents lawsuits, agents of every type, need help creating a distinguishing value proposition

149

ANCILLARY BUSINESS PROFESSIONALS

CPA's, Financial Planners and Attorneys, are all hyper focused on doing what they do well. If we have a unique approach to our business and we can show them how we will be an incredibly valuable partner, they would be fortunate to work with mortgage professionals like us because it will improve their business and their clients' livelihoods.

I have a standing bet with our group, that if anyone meets with one of these professionals, presents their unique value proposition and commits to helping them, I will pay $100 if they don't get the opportunity to partner. I have never paid that bet…

OTHER MORTGAGE PROFESSIONALS

The great thing about believing in our product and seeing all of the benefits that come with it, is that other mortgage professionals see it and they need what we do, badly. This gives all of us the opportunity to help others, in a leadership position, as our industry will continue to struggle on a race to the bottom. In a market where cheaper options are always available, standing out requires a focus on the value that only we can provide. Cheaper doesn't always mean better, especially when it comes to significant life decisions and the outcome of one's financial success. We will earn the opportunity to attract and help others, which is an incredibly fulfilling feeling.

As we start to implement this new version of mortgage lending, we have to realize that we're going to inevitably face obstacles. The best way to overcome those obstacles is…you guessed in, BELIEF!! Our belief is communicated not just in what we say but HOW we say it.

Clients are perceptive and can distinguish between genuine conviction and a sales pitch. When we discuss our product's features, we have to frame them in terms of how they benefit the client, addressing their needs and concerns. Our enthusiasm, confidence, and sincerity are infectious and can often be the deciding factor in a client's choice. Every sales professional encounters objections. However, when we genuinely believe in the value of our product, we can address these objections not as roadblocks but as opportunities to further explain the value of what we're offering. Understanding and believing in the nuances of our product equips us to provide solutions that competitors simply can't match.

CASE STUDY: BELIEF IN ACTION

One of our team members, named Justin, was a seasoned loan officer who had been in the business for about six years before joining our group. He was doing pretty good business but was struggling with what made him unique to his clients and his business partners. He was inspired to change what he was offering and worked tirelessly on implementing the entire new holistic product offering into his business. In doing so, he not only started to improve, but he legitimately now believes that he will help his clients and partners in ways that others just simply will not. Not only is he thriving, but he had his best year ever, in 2023, after being in the business for seven years.

BELIEF, AUTHENTICITY, TEAM ENGAGEMENT AND CONTINUOUS IMPROVEMENT

Believing in our product (which again, is ourselves, our knowledge and the totality of what we offer our clients), is a mindset that can be nurtured and developed. We must stay informed about industry changes, share our client success stories, and take note of the broader impact of our work.

Our team needs to understand and buy into the unique value proposition as well, as this will come through in their interactions with clients. When our team sincerely believes in the product, they'll communicate with authenticity and passion, which is infectious and persuasive. We have to stay engaged and teach/lead our teams and clients to continually reinforce the real-world benefits of our product. Remember, our belief is a powerful tool in our arsenal, capable of turning challenges into successes and skeptics into advocates. Also, and most importantly, this belief isn't just about confidence in the product's features; it's about believing in the positive impact it can have on our clients' lives.

Once we've developed our differentiated offering, the work isn't over. The market and client needs will continue to evolve, and so should our product. We have to implement a system for continuous feedback from clients and frontline staff. This will allow us to make iterative improvements, further refining and distinguishing our offering in the marketplace.

CONCLUSION

Believing in our product is not just a sales strategy; it's a core principle of being a successful mortgage professional. It's about understanding the profound impact a home, combined with proactive advice and guidance, can have on a person's life and conveying that understanding with every interaction. When we believe in our product, we're not just selling a mortgage; we're providing a service before, during and after the mortgage transaction, that can change lives. Our belief is our signature, our promise, and ultimately, our most compelling selling point against cheaper competitors.

It's not about being different for the sake of it; it's about being better in a way that meaningfully impacts our clients' lives. As we transform our product offering, we'll not only enhance our competitive edge but also become a trusted partner in our clients' journey toward financial freedom and creating real generational wealth.

CHAPTER 19:
Reignite your career with Ideas and Action

Here's the understatement of the century: the mortgage industry has evolved DRAMATICALLY. Loan Officers find themselves in a rapidly evolving environment that demands a change in approach to business development. In the past, we could rely on our past customer database and a handful of Real Estate agent partnerships for referrals. To thrive in today's market, Mortgage Professionals must diversify their sources of business and take a multilayered approach that combines traditional methods with a modern system.

This chapter will look at critical focus areas for Mortgage Professionals looking to grow their business in the new mortgage market.

Additionally, to help Loan Officers initiate their evolution, I've written an eBook called '22 *Business Development Ideas for Loan Officers.*' More on this later... for now, I'll set the stage.

1) Additional Pillars for Additional Opportunities

Traditionally, Loan Officers have relied on existing relationships with past clients and realtors. While this is still a valuable pillar of business, it is no longer enough in a market that requires that we have more lead sources. In short, we need more fishing lines in the water. At this time, I'm recommending 5-10 reliable business sources. This mitigates risk, ensures a steady flow of leads, and keeps you from scrambling when one business source runs dry. Here are just a few ideas.

- *Financial Planners* – Collaborating with productive financial advisors can lead to a steady stream of quality referrals. They have a loyal client base that is well-qualified, financially savvy, and ready for home ownership. This is especially valuable in a refinance cycle.

- *Renovation Niche'* – Renovation lending can provide a big lift when housing inventory is low. There is an opportunity to market to sellers, buyers, and Business Partners in this niche.

- *FSBO listings*– Every seller needs a new mortgage, and their potential buyers also need help with financing. As a plus, many FSBOs eventually hire a realtor, allowing you to refer these individuals to a Real Estate Agent.

- *Networking Groups* – Networking groups, like BNI, provide connections to local leaders committed to sharing connections and referring business.

2) Building an Authentic Digital Presence

In a world where digital communication is king, Mortgage Professionals must leverage social media platforms to establish and build authentic personal brands, showcase success stories, and share informative content. In this space, authenticity is key, where people are drawn to genuine personalities. And keep in mind that a sprinkle of fun can go a long way in connecting with people. Here are crucial elements to consider:

- *Social Media presence.* Maintain active LinkedIn, Facebook, YouTube, Instagram, and TikTok profiles. Share content that educates the reader about mortgages and gives insight into who you are as a person. Authenticity resonates with audiences and builds trust.

- *Video content.* Use video content to convey your unique skills and personality. Create informative videos about mortgage processes and industry trends and answer common financing questions. Also, share pieces of your daily life to connect with clients personally.

- *Digital relationship building.* Even in the digital world, relationships matter. Engage with your audience through likes, comments, and direct messages. Interacting with people you would like to meet makes them feel they should return the favor and engage with your content. Responding promptly and thoughtfully creates a sense that you are approachable and accessible.

3) Consumer direct marketing strategies

An effective consumer direct marketing strategy ensures you have opportunities to refer to your business partners. Loyalty is earned when business flows in both directions. Here are a few practical ways to connect with consumers directly:

- ***Rate Watch Content.*** Write content that educates consumers about market trends, interest rate changes, and the potential to refinance into a lower rate. This positions you as a reliable and valuable source of information.

- ***Educational Webinars and Workshops.*** Host webinars and workshops to educate potential clients about the mortgage process, financial planning, and homeownership. Establish yourself as a vital resource, and your audience will turn to you when ready for their next home purchase or refinance.

4) Filling the coaching GAP.

As the squeeze on profit margins continues, loan officers often lack the support they need for business planning, business development, and accountability. Some sales leaders have been pushed out of the industry, and many others have become focused on administrative duties and recruiting. This leaves Mortgage Professionals to navigate the mortgage landscape independently or seek external coaching. Unfortunately, external coaching can be expensive, and the nuances of the individual mortgage company may not be fully understood.

Here are three tips to help mortgage professionals succeed, even if they are in the coaching gap:

Business Development ideas. Recognizing the coaching gap, I have written an eBook titled, '22 Business Development Ideas for Mortgage Pros.' The book aims to fill the void by providing Mortgage Professionals with diverse ideas to generate leads and increase business. This will be a great starting point. Please scan the QR code to learn how to get a free copy of the ebook.

2 **Develop a Business Plan.** Mortgage Professionals must take the ideas presented in the eBook and develop them into a personalized business plan. One that focuses on results and considers your strengths and personal goals.

3 **Consistent and Persistent Action.** Success as a Mortgage Professional requires more than ideas and a plan; it demands consistent and persistent action. Implementing the ideas outlined in the eBook requires daily discipline, dedication, and an ongoing commitment to building and nurturing online AND offline relationships.

In conclusion, the mortgage industry has undergone massive changes, and loan officers must change their business development strategies accordingly. Mortgage Professionals can position themselves for success by

- Increasing professional networks,
- Creating an authentic digital presence,
- Implementing consumer direct marketing strategies,
- Navigating the coaching gap by taking action on new ideas.

Adopting an approach that combines traditional marketing methods with modern advances is the key to thriving in this competitive world of the mortgage business.

CHAPTER 20:
The Power of Education

As all great Navy stories start out: There I was.... sitting in my office in Honolulu, Hawaii on Pearl Harbor Naval Base. I was the acting Commanding Officer, because my boss happened to be on travel at the time. It was a beautiful sunny day, but I had no time to take notice because I was up to my chin in paperwork. About 1330 (that's 1:30pm for you civilians), one of my junior sailors walked into my office and said "sir, we have a guy coming here to talk to us about VA Home Loans."

Immediately, I said "No, you can't do that." He looked at me being briefly dazed and said "Sir, he's going to be here in 15 minutes."

Understand that when you are in command, one of your primary objectives is the protection of the people that are placed under your care. My primary concern was that someone would come in and convince my sailors to do something that was not in their best interest or "sell" them something. We couldn't cancel the presentation at that point in the day so I did the only thing that I could do. I put all my work on pause, and decided to sit in this presentation, just to ensure that nothing was said to coerce my sailors.

It was an hour and a half that would change the course of my life. I was on course to be the Commanding Officer of my own naval warship. It would be the culmination of a 20+ year career. But it was in those 90 minutes the course of my life changed. I sat there as Tony Dias, the man who would later help me enter the mortgage industry, educated us about the power of the VA home loan benefit. Although I had used my VA home loan to purchase my first home, my eyes were opened to the information that many veterans did not know about VA home loans and the fact that it can be used to build wealth! At the end of the presentation, I walked up to the presenter and said, "When it's time for me to retire, I would be happy to work with you". He happily obliged, but I did not know that the time would come sooner rather than later.

In the following months, the presentation ran over in my mind repeatedly. It was not the information particularly, but the fact that he stood there, and he educated us. He did not talk about debt-to-income ratio, underwriting guidelines, and all the boring aspects of mortgage. He spoke to us as active-duty service members and veterans, and talked about how this could change our lives. Eventually, I did call Tony and I retired from the military and immediately got into mortgages. In fact, I spent my last nine months on active duty doing mortgages...... and I was very good at doing them. Was it because I understood underwriting, title, or even residual income on a VA loan?

Absolutely not!

I did understand that if people are educated, they make more educated decisions about homeownership. So, I focused on education.

In my third month as a mortgage loan originator, I closed 16 units and I have never closed less than 100 units in a single year. I don't say that to impress you, I say that so that you understand the power of education. As an originator, you should understand that if you take just a part of this strategy and execute it consistently, it has the power to change your business, change your life, and more importantly, the lives of others.

First things first. You are not a processor, you are not a loan officer assistant, and you are not an underwriter. While you should know what these people do as a part of the mortgage process, your focus should be to generate mortgage opportunities, or what people in our business will refer to as "lead generation". But it is not enough to generate a lead. You need that person to be connected to you and connect to your "voice" so that they heed your advice, and then they direct other people to you because you gave them information and knowledge to help them make the right decision. In fact, you need to be at peace adding value and education EVEN WHEN YOU DO NOT DO THAT PERSON'S LOAN. If you sow, I GUARANTEE you will reap.

Now, I know what you're asking. How do I get in front of people to create these mortgage opportunities? There are two methods. The first method is to educate the educator. Believe it, or not, most realtors know very little about loan products and everyone loves a "catchy" training topic. While the writing of this book, I am teaching two classes to realtors. The first is "Everything realtors need to know about VA loans" the second is "Recession Protection: How to do more business with less buyers." I usually have about 20-25 realtors in each one of these classes.

For the VA class, we've taken the extra step of getting CE accredited which draws a little more people, further, it positions me as an expert on the VA home loan. Your next question would be "Major, where do I teach these classes?" The answer to that question is quite simple. Title companies! This is because they are the only people that want to be in front of realtors more than you. Partner with the title companies to teach classes at their facilities. They invite their database and use their influence to get people into the class. I like to offer lunch, which is usually coordinated between me and Title Company at an extremely low cost. The return on investment is huge for both me and the title company. For more information on how this is formatted and tips on how to construct your training, scan the QR code here.

 The second method is to educate the buyer. Who are the only people that want to be in front of buyers more than you do? Realtors! Partner with the realtors (ideally the ones you met at your training session with the title company) to do a homebuying workshop.

Typically, these workshops are smaller and more intimate. You may do this at a bookstore, coffee shop, title company (if you have a large group), or an apartment complex club house. It gives you a chance to do a buyer's consultation while giving knowledge about the homebuying process. Again, your education and knowledge will be on display as you become the source, and the buyers will continuously run to you so that you can walk them through the process while also sending their family and friends to you to help them buy homes.

Here is the ideal flow that you want to develop......

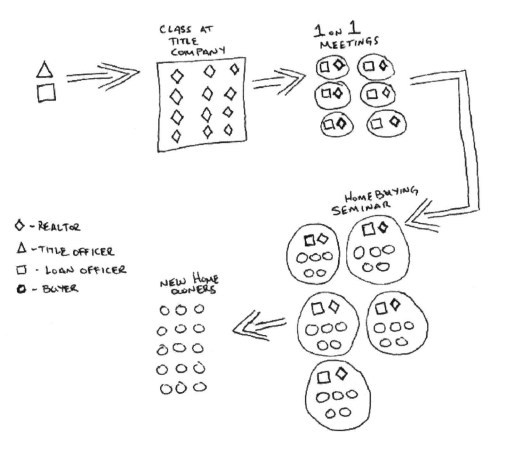

If you're going to rethink everything, you know about being a loan officer, it starts with understanding that you are not a loan officer who happens to educate people. You are an educator, who happens to be a loan officer. When people ask what I do for a living, I often say that I am a very highly compensated educator. If you can reformat your thinking to be an educator and then determine how to get your educational tools in front of the most amount of people, there is nothing stopping you from being a successful originator in this market, or in any market.

Now, *go win!*

CHAPTER 21:
Michael Jordan, Neurosurgeons, and a Bad Boss

Do you ever see successful people and wonder how they got to where they are at? By successful, I mean they are at the top tier of their profession. Lets take, for example Tiger Woods, and what kind of an impact he made on golf. He specialized in all aspects of one particular sport – golf. He did not try to go pro in football, basketball, or tennis. Nope, he said I am good at golf, I love golf, and I will be the best at GOLF.

Same for Tom Brady, he chose to specialize in Football and specifically at quarterback, which narrowed his specialization even further from just working on being the best football player to being the best quarterback in football.

Michael Jordan, Lionel Messi, Wayne Gretzky, Kobe Bryant, Mike Tyson....you get the point. They were passionate about becoming the best in their specific space and dedicated all aspects of their lives to accentuate, elevate, and separate themselves from others in their same field. Sports is an easy one to see this in, but this would go for any profession in the world. Lets look at the medical field. You have a general practitioner, then you have a surgeon, but then it can get even more narrow. You start into the specialist arena– neurosurgeon, thoracic surgeon, or an ophthalmologist. They had a passion for the medical field, but then saw an opportunity within themselves and dedicated even more time to be one of the few that specialize in one very specific thing.

Hopefully, I am painting the picture to my question – how did successful people get to where they are at? Simply put – they chose to specialize and be extraordinary in their field. They chose what they do intentionally and poured their life into becoming whom we see them to be today. Far too often, people say, "well that person is just a gifted athlete and it is easy for them to do that" or "they just come from a successful background and were just given the position." I've thought this, you've thought this, and I bet someone reading this right now is doing this at this very moment – their coworker, their competitor, or teammate didn't earn or deserve what they have but somehow I DO. I think I know why we do this...its an excuse we give ourselves!

Aint it easier to justify this excuse or reasoning on someone who is successful, rather than acknowledging what hard work, effort, and sacrifices they made to get there?

Because if we actually acknowledged the hard work put into it, then we would become cognizant of what it took to get there. Well, that sounds too hard now and we like to be cozy and content because...who wants to work hard and sacrifice?

I almost forgot that this is a book I was asked to help write a chapter for my good friends Kyle and Brian for the next generation of loan officers! These guys are phenomenal, extremely gifted, and absolutely nuts for asking ME to write about anything.

Seriously, me? Who would want to read what I have to say? Yall would be better off asking Kyle and Brian on the countless amazing and inspiring accomplishments they've done. Kyle approached me and said: You are very accomplished, blessed, and successful in the mortgage space as it relates to servicing builders. Write about that buddy! Well, there is that word again, "successful." I seriously don't ever refer to myself as this. I think it is rather weird when people speak of themselves like that. But as I was writing this for you, I noticed that similar to some of the people I mentioned earlier in my chapter, I chose a very specific sector of the lending industry to specialize in: **Builder Business.**

A little background on me with this. I spent my first 10 years working for a mortgage company that was 100% focused on servicing builders with their lending needs. They partnered with big private and publicly held builders forming affiliated business arrangements and producing joint ventures. For the first couple of years, I was just there making GOOD money. I was 23 years old, working 60-70 hours a week, 7 days a week, and unintentionally learning a lot.

Then I heard some wise words, from a boss who I am very thankful for but… at speaking engagements will center a whole topic I am covering for my presentation around the theme of the "bad boss" I had back in the day. Will talk about this at length one day when I write a book on leadership – The Do's and Don'ts When You Accidently Become the Boss….Kyle and Brian will contribute to my book in return for this.

So my boss at the mortgage company said to me, "You know why I love builders, Michael? Because, if rates are low then builders sell a lot of homes. And when rates are high, builders still sell a lot of homes." That struck me.

This is a good thing for me to get in deep with as it has lasting power and market insulation. Then I thought to myself: Don't just get good at doing builder business, get excellent at it. Become an expert. Dig in and soak this all up while learning with bad boss at the builder centric mortgage company, with my low overhead (23 years old at the time and man I miss how cheap it was to live!), and learn everything I could on both sides of the business. Learn everything on the lending side and learn all aspects of how it relates to support the builder.

I learned builders will always have a need for lenders. Over the next several years, it was proven what bad boss told me, rates went up and builders still sold a lot of homes. It was a lot of work supporting and learning all things builder related but guess what, I loved learning and it paid off, big time.

Most of my peers in the lending space, just wanted the easy fast money. Therefore, very few people entered this builder lender space and the exclusivity served me well!

If I were to start over again, I would intentionally learn all about builder again and again find someone to mentor me.

It is my firm belief that being a "jack of all trades and a master of none" is what holds back the majority of us in the lender space from true success. Here is my advice for you – find a specialized sector of the lending space with this core criteria: Will always be needed. A profitable business model or loan product. That intrigues and fuels you in learning about it. Then immerse yourself in becoming an expert in that sector. Examples other than builder business include: Reverse Mortgages, Self Employed Borrowers, Alternative or Alt A Products, or Jumbo Loans to name a few. As for finding the mentor, that would be anyone that you discover is already where you want to get at and it just could be a bad boss you need for a time being to learn from too!

CHAPTER 22:
The Art of The Sale

WELCOME TO THE ART OF THE SALE!

Look People In The Eyes:

How often does the little voice in your head prompt you to say something and you never speak those words out loud? Maybe you're talking to the agent sitting across from you at coffee? Or to that new lead on the phone comparing options (who was referred to you and two others)? Maybe it's something that needs to be said to your employees? Looking people in the eyes today is more about speaking out loud the words YOU have going on in your head, but that most people are not willing to say out loud. Things like:

"You're probably thinking that every loan officer in town wants to have coffee with you, and yet none add value. If I were you, I'd be thinking that too."

"If I were you, I'd be shopping everywhere to find what I consider is the best deal, but it's hard to say that to those who you speak with."

"I want to give you a raise but am concerned that if I do, you'll just leave in six months. How do I protect my company and make you feel valued?"

Speaking into what you or others are thinking AND then addressing it creatively and honestly is one of the most important skills our generation has lost. We've become too soft and passive.

Being direct isn't rude. Being honest isn't either. Speaking into the space of assumption that we all have is a skill we all need to practice more.

Commit to speaking the "*voice*". Start today…

Call everyone you have refinanced lately and explain the realities of an EPO. Explain how the industry works and address what you would be doing (in their shoes) if you had an interest rate you hoped to refi out of. Then offer a creative solution. Try it on with authenticity.

Send a video to an agent you've followed online and hope to work with. Tell them why their time won't be wasted meeting with you and then address what you know that voice in their head is telling them about Loan Officers. You aren't average so it's okay to speak about those who are.

Sit down with your team. Share your biggest fears in business that you don't think they would understand. Ask them to share theirs. You will be shocked how close this brings your team.

Your biggest crutch and potential differentiator:

Our greatest curse and one of our greatest potential advantages is technology.

My dad loved technology. He was that "guy" to buy the first CD player. He leveraged technology to engage his mind and create opportunities for story and community. He did not use it to cut corners.

Far too often I see people using technology to cut corners. They buy tools that they don't learn to use and never fully implement. I have been there and done that! It is not a recipe for success.

Those we look to as winners, top sales leaders and entrepreneurs leverage a few key technologies with religious consistency.

First, They OWN their data. If you don't have a CRM that can send email, text and sort all data simply and easily, STOP investing in any other technology right now. There are hundreds of companies right now focused solely on acquiring data. They know that consumer data is one of the keys to future revenue. One of your main competitors recently purchased a money management app for over $1,000,000,000. Human spending patterns and potential client data has more value than ever before. And yet you have that data and throw it away?

Those who have mastered technology, also authentically communicate via video. My dad didn't have this tool at his disposal in the 1970's. He had to fly to Dubai to start a negotiation. We can now communicate with potential clients or referral partners via video. And many people prefer it!

Get your data in order. Then create an authentic video communication based on the information your CRM now has sorted and organized. Use video to relay your message specifically and generally.

One of the best ways I have found to speak to individuals, directly is through one to one videos.

In addition to having more authentic conversations with individuals, grab a yellow notepad and for the next 60 days write down every question asked by your audience. Then each time it's asked again put a ✓ next to it. Those frequently asked conversations then get answered in generic, evergreen videos you can repurpose. Record them speaking generally and share them on YouTube. Then repurpose those videos on all other social platforms (Try the Ask, Answered Technique). Feeling bold? Cut them up into short form content and you are now compressing time!

This leads to my last thought and one you can finally leverage effectively if you have dialed in communication and technology.

TRUE COMMUNITY

One thing we all want is community. My dad was the master at creating community. He "broke bread" with everyone he came into contact with. When he entered the room, you knew it. Not because he was arrogant or a blow hard, but because he was just authentically himself and blessed everyone with his time and generosity.

Today you can do this too.

Imagine if you had a free platform you could leverage to share authentic stories, vulnerable moments of weakness, times of triumph, neighborhood updates, summarize the news that mattered and more. And you could do this in about 15 minutes a day?

We already have this available and yet most of us simply fumble through it with no clear plan of attack to get our brand in front of our audience.

The problem is not that we can't be heard. The problem is we don't know what to say.

Far too often we use social media to turn off our brains. We mindlessly thumb through Facebook comparing our real life to others' fake lives. Then we remember that our competition is leveraging social media for work and we end up posting crappy and typically overused content to feel like we are keeping up with our competition.

What if instead of losing slowly, we won authentically?

What if for the next 30 days you posted twice a day a combination of the following?

- what made you happy?
- what made you sad?
- what is happening locally?
- what is impacting your audience right now?
- what is funny and made you laugh?
- what made you think deeply?
- what you are struggling through but have a solution for?
- what changes are impacting your industry?
- what is free and available to your audience that you feel would benefit them?
- what you read or heard that was impactful?

Include images or videos you recorded and words you wrote.

Ignore what your competition is doing.

While doing this, add ANYONE you know, want to know or need to know.

Engage with their content with purpose and authenticity.

Set a 5 minute timer and do this 3 or 4 times a day so you don't get lost in social media black holes!

You will be amazed and surprised at how much your audience will get to know the real you. Not the false "you" that you think people will judge, but the real and authentic YOU.

This isn't just highly effective in sales, it's also much easier to manage doing since it's just you being you.

Spoiler alert! The Art of the Sale has little to do with the sale.

How we operate, what we leverage and the purpose behind our actions is the foundation that creates a sales process so easy it won't be fair to our competitors. They won't stand a chance when the version of you that looks everyone in the eyes, leverages a few technologies at a high level and fosters true community, walks into the room.

Serving Others w/ Education & Advocacy

Presented by:

My CreditGuy
CREDIT RESTORATION

This section shines a light on the transformative power of knowledge and the pivotal role of advocacy in the real estate finance industry.

The writers each underscore the importance of continuous education and the active engagement in advocacy to bridge the knowledge gap between professionals, policymakers, and consumers we serve. Through personal anecdotes and professional insights, it illustrates how mastering one's craft and leveraging knowledge not only elevates individual careers but also significantly impacts veterans and other homebuyers. It champions the idea that true service extends beyond transactions, emphasizing the duty to educate, advocate, and empower, thereby enriching the homebuying journey for all stakeholders.

CHAPTER 23:
Industry Advocacy

The real estate finance industry operates in a complex environment shaped by economic, legislative, regulatory, and societal factors. Policies related to taxation, interest rates, housing affordability, and foreclosure prevention have direct implications. A significant challenge faced by professionals in this field is the limited understanding by legislators on the federal, state, and local levels about its intricacies.

Loan officers (LOs), being at the forefront of the industry, must recognize this knowledge gap and actively engage in industry advocacy efforts.

Advocacy is essential in the policymaking process as it allows loan officers to create positive changes by educating decision-makers and driving legislation. Continuous communication and storytelling between individuals/constituents of the mortgage industry and government entities is a key component of effective advocacy.

By choice or default, we all operate in the political arena. Whether it's curbing the abusive use of trigger leads or advancing programs that reduce barriers to homeownership and support the American dream, what happens in Washington, D.C. or your state capital affects your business and your bottom line. Industry trade organizations provide industry professionals with a path to have their voices heard.

There are many ways to participate in advocacy in our industry. The National Mortgage Bankers Association (MBA) is YOUR resource for all things advocacy. MBA is the industry's leading trade organization, serving its members through a comprehensive array of capabilities and tools that enable members to successfully deliver fair, sustainable, and responsible real estate financing within ever-changing business environments. With a dedicated team of policy and advocacy experts, MBA drives legislation and regulation to ensure your business can operate at its full potential. While the staff at MBA can rightly take credit for some of that success, it wouldn't have the same effect without active engagement and participation from its advocates.

 MBA staff regularly meets with key members of Congress to educate them on the needs of your businesses but, to make the largest impact, policymakers need to hear your story directly from you, their constituents.

MBA advocates year-round on the industry's behalf, but you are an expert in the field. Together we can stay informed, get engaged, and be able to influence further change.

The Mortgage Action Alliance (MAA) is the Mortgage Bankers Association (MBA)'s FREE grassroots advocacy network. MAA is a tool for industry professionals to speak directly to policymakers at the federal and state levels when important legislation is up  for debate. Having regular contact with your lawmakers and their staff members through MAA's Calls to Action is critical to ensure your elected officials understand how policy issues affect you, your customers, and the communities you serve.

Join MAA, MBA's army of advocates, and help protect the future of the industry. The larger the group, the louder the voice!

CHAPTER 24:
capital Markets

Always remain teachable. If you're reading this book, we already know you want to learn, but there is a huge difference between being learned and teachable. John Maxwell has a great article from 2011 that demonstrates how to maintain a teachable attitude. I highly recommend the quick read.

This one is very personal for me because most of my career I have been very teachable, and you guessed it, I've grown exponentially, but there have been moments when I was not, because I thought I had it all figured out, and you guessed again, I suffered because I robbed myself of the growth I could have had in those periods of my life.

I've been in the mortgage industry for 15 years now. Hired in at the end of 2008 (that was a weird time). I was fortunate enough to start my career in the capital markets space with a hedge advisory firm. A hedge advisory firm is essentially a capital markets department for hire. We traded loans, created pools, hedged, provided pricing models, ran analytics, and advised our clients on how to maximize their execution which led to higher revenue and the ability to offer better rates. We did this for almost 40 well known banks and mortgage companies. Starting my career this way gave me a really unique perspective of the industry and how it functions. Crazy to think that some of the largest mortgage lending institutions would not exist without these functions and the robust secondary market we have.

While working at the hedge advisory firm I never spoke to Loan Officers. On our client side my conversations were always with the head of secondary marketing or capital markets department, the CFO or the owner of the company. It wasn't until I joined a mid-sized mortgage lender that I started speaking with the sales teams and holy crap…I was in over my head. Not because I didn't know my stuff from a capital markets perspective but because I had never had to explain it to someone that didn't already know what I was talking about. I had to completely rethink what I knew and how to explain it in a way that Loan Officers, Realtors and the general public could understand. Because after all, the "market" drives everything we do in the business right down to our pay checks as I'm sure we've all felt throughout 2022 and 2023.

As I got to know my sales staff, I started to notice that many of them didn't have a grasp on what was going on in the market, how loans were sold or how their rate sheets came to be and that's because many of them either didn't care or they thought they knew enough. I would get comments like, "I don't need to know that stuff, that's your job."

But of course, there were a few that did get it. And while maybe they didn't know what a buy up and buy down grid was (buy up and buy down grids are part of an equation that help us decide which coupon we should slot certain interest rates into), they were curious and inquisitive. They started their mornings watching financial news, they subscribed to market commentary, and other housing news outlets. They created a network of people that they deemed smarter than themselves on this topic. But most importantly, they were consistent. They monitored what was happening in the market and housing industry every day. They considered it one of their most important time blocks. And wouldn't you know it, they were some of our top producers.

One thing these LO's never did was rely on a single source for information. There are some great resources out there. Some will even tell you if you should lock your loans now or later. The only issue is if they're wrong, you as the originator end up with egg on you face, not them. Don't let someone else do your homework for you because you will fail the test. Some of my favorite resources are Bloomberg News, HousingWire News, The Mortgage Bankers Association, and the last paragraph of Rob Chrisman's Blog. My absolute favorite is the broker dealer commentary. If your company hedges, they work with a number of broker dealers. You can ask your head of capital markets to add you the distribution list for the commentary. And if you're anything like me, when you first start reading it you won't understand it. Google and Investopedia will be your best friends.

Now let's talk about the pandemic...where everyone became a student of the market overnight. We all thought the world was ending. On one hand it was scary has hell, on the other, it was an incredible opportunity for the entire industry to learn how the market and economy really drives everything we do.

Here are the top three reason being a student of the market can help with your business.

1. **You become proactive vs. reactive.** While understanding the driving forces of the market and consistently taking in the information does not give you a crystal ball, it does help you see things that may affect your business before your competition who is likely not paying attention.

2. **You actually have something of value to give to your referral partners and clients.** I'm sure you've had several referral partners come to you over the last two years and ask what the heck is going on with the market and interest rates. So instead of B.S.-ing your way through it you can become their go to expert.

3. **Lastly, it helps open your mind to the bigger picture.** This will help you negotiate better on your own behalf and ultimately run a better business.

So again, being learned isn't enough. Remain teachable and open to new ways to differentiate yourself. It will not only help you become a better originator but likely a better person.

CHAPTER 25:
credit Expertise

This book and the opportunity to contribute came at just the right time for me.

I was forced to *rethink everything* after November 1, 2022, when I received the lay off call so many of us in the Mortgage Industry had been receiving.

#sueknowsthescore was born on November 8th, and what you'll find in this chapter and videos are my passion project coming to life.

In the ever-evolving landscape of real estate, the role of a Loan officer Advisor goes beyond mere transactional processes. Today's loan advisors are becoming catalysts for change, guiding potential home-buyers not just through the complexities of financing but also empowering them with the knowledge to become successful homeowners. One key element of this transformative approach is credit empowerment – a focus that positions loan advisors as advocates for their clients' success as homeowners, not just a home-buyer.

This requires a rethinking of everything you thought you knew about credit.

UNDERSTANDING THE POWER OF CREDIT EMPOWERMENT:

Credit empowerment is more than just a buzzword; it's a philosophy that recognizes the significance of informed financial decisions. As a next-generation loan advisor, your role extends beyond the traditional confines of mortgage approval. You become a mentor, a guide, and a partner in your clients' journey towards credit excellence.

My own journey to credit empowerment started in the Mortgage Industry, but on the Credit Reseller side.

In the mid 1980's we weren't approving buyers in days, it took weeks.

Some credit reports still fit on 3x5 cards, and the idea of credit empowerment, credit literacy and credit education, specifically for a Loan Officer was decades away.

The path to home ownership for everyone starts with a credit pull. Lack of guidance for your home buyers in this very first step by you could be the difference between success and failure. For you and for them.

Be the difference. Be the mentor, partner and guide your home buyers deserve for this life-changing journey of homeownership.

Simplifying and Humanizing complex credit concepts:

Let's face it, credit is boring. BORING. Unless you are rocking an 800+ credit score, it's all about how to get better. It's our job to make the borrowers perfect score attainable. Not the perfect score, their perfect score.

The first step towards credit empowerment is breaking down the complex concepts surrounding credit. Many potential home-buyers are intimidated by credit scores, credit reports, and the intricacies of financial health. Many are fearful, or maybe ashamed of past credit issues. Humanize the process for them.

As a loan advisor, you can distinguish yourself by crafting content that uses plain language, relatable analogies, and real-life examples to make credit education accessible to a broader audience.

Leveraging Referrals and content creators:

While you may not consider yourself a credit expert, you can still position yourself as a credit empowerment advocate. Build a strong network of credit specialists and financial educators who can complement your services. Referring clients to these experts or collaborating with content creators to develop informative materials can enhance your credibility and provide valuable resources for your clients.

Keeping up on all the newest changes in mortgage lending is a task for anyone, having trusted resources will be key to the next-generation loan advisor.

2 BUILDING A FOUNDATION FOR SUCCESSFUL HOME BUYERS TO BECOME SUCCESSFUL HOMEOWNERS:

Empowering your clients with credit knowledge is the foundation for creating successful home buyers. A well-informed buyer is not only better equipped to navigate the home buying process but is also more likely to secure favorable financing terms. When you become the Loan Advisor that helped them secure a lower interest rate, better PMI terms and a more affordable monthly payment, you will reap the rewards with referrals. Here are key strategies to achieve this:

Facilitating Access to Financial Tools:

Empower homeowners with tools that simplify financial management. This could include budgeting apps, credit monitoring services, or resources for understanding and managing their mortgage.

By giving them the tools to take control of their financial well-being, you contribute to the creation of successful, self-sufficient homeowners.

3 FOSTERING SUCCESSFUL HOMEOWNERSHIP THROUGH CREDIT WELLNESS:

Once your clients have successfully transitioned from potential homebuyers to homeowners, your role as a credit empowerment advocate does not end. To ensure sustained success, focus on fostering credit wellness throughout their homeownership journey:

Offering Financial Literacy Workshops:

Host workshops or webinars that cover topics such as budgeting, managing debt, and building wealth. Providing ongoing financial education helps homeowners make informed decisions, preventing potential financial pitfalls and contributing to the overall stability of their homeownership experience.

Celebrating Financial Milestones:

Acknowledge and celebrate your clients' financial milestones. Whether it's paying off a significant portion of their mortgage, improving their credit score, or achieving other financial goals, recognizing their achievements fosters a positive relationship and reinforces the value you bring as a credit empowerment advocate.

Conclusion:

In the dynamic world of real estate, the next-generation loan advisor has the opportunity to be a positive force in clients' lives by embracing credit empowerment. By positioning yourself as an advocate, simplifying credit concepts, and fostering ongoing financial education, you can create a community of successful homebuyers and homeowners. Remember, it's not just about facilitating a transaction; it's about empowering individuals to achieve their dreams and build a strong foundation for a financially secure future.

CHAPTER 26:
understanding The veteran Mindset

As a seasoned professional in the housing industry, my experiences with veteran homebuyers have profoundly shaped my understanding of their unique needs and challenges.

Veterans, having served our country, come into the home buying process with a distinct mindset shaped by their service experiences. They're not just looking for a house; they're seeking stability, trust, and a sense of community.

In my journey, I've learned that the greatest obstacle in serving our veterans effectively isn't just market dynamics or financial intricacies, but a profound gap in understanding and knowledge among many housing professionals.

UNDERSTANDING THE VETERAN MINDSET

Veterans approach home buying differently than civilian consumers. Their experiences, often marked by constant changes and a high level of adaptability, breed a natural skepticism towards processes and systems. This skepticism can manifest as reluctance to share crucial information if they sense a lack of expertise or understanding from their real estate professionals. To effectively serve veterans, it's crucial to understand this mindset. It begins with recognizing their specific needs and the intricacies of VA loans, which are often misunderstood or underutilized due to misconceptions in the industry.

BUILDING TRUST
THROUGH EXPERTISE AND PROBLEM-SOLVING

In real estate, trust is the cornerstone of any successful transaction. With veterans, this trust is established not through sales tactics or competitive rates, but through the demonstration of genuine expertise and problem-solving skills. Veterans are more likely to engage and share important details when they feel confident in a professional's knowledge and ability to address their unique challenges. This trust-building is about being seen not just as a service provider, but as a knowledgeable and reliable partner in their homebuying journey.

THE ART OF SELLING:
PROBLEM SOLVING, NOT PERSUASION

Effective selling within the context of VA housing shifts the focus from persuasion to problem-solving. Every interaction with a veteran homebuyer is an opportunity to face new challenges and provide solutions. When a veteran realizes that you can solve problems no one else has been able to, they naturally gravitate towards your services. This approach transforms the nature of sales into a relationship built on trust and expertise, where the veteran's needs are the primary focus.

THE NEED FOR ADVOCACY AND CONTINUOUS EDUCATION

Advocacy and education are paramount in the profession of serving veteran homebuyers. Understanding the latest in VA loans, their capabilities, and how they can best serve veterans requires continuous learning. It's about going beyond the basics and delving deep into resources like the VA handbook and other guidelines to offer accurate and timely solutions. As professionals, our moral obligation extends beyond transactions; we are advocates for veterans and their entitlements, understanding their unique financial challenges and the opportunities that VA loans provide.

PERSONAL JOURNEY: FROM MARINE TO MORTGAGE PROFESSIONAL

My personal journey from the Marine Corps to navigating the complex world of VA loans has deeply influenced my approach to this profession. When I purchased my first home using a VA loan, it wasn't just a financial decision; it was a life-changing moment for my family, offering stability, a sense of belonging, and an opportunity to finally set down roots. This personal experience has been a driving force in my commitment to ensuring every veteran receives the respect, knowledge, and service they deserve.

THE PATH TO PROFICIENCY

Becoming proficient in serving veterans requires a fundamental shift in our professional approach. It's about being an effective problem solver, an empathetic listener, and a knowledgeable advisor. Our goal should be to understand the unique situations veterans face and offer solutions that resonate with their needs and aspirations. We must rise above viewing veterans as just another market segment; they're individuals who have made significant sacrifices and deserve our utmost respect and dedication.

Serving veterans in the housing market is an honor and a responsibility. It demands more than just technical knowledge; it requires a deep understanding of their experiences, a commitment to continuous learning, and a genuine desire to advocate for their best interests. By adopting this approach, we not only enhance our professional capabilities but also contribute positively to the lives of those who have bravely served our nation.

Veterans, when approaching the homebuying process, often look for professionals who can lead with confidence and provide substantial support, not just sales pitches. They value professionals who can guide them through the complexities of homebuying with authority and understanding. Veterans have been conditioned to respect and follow strong leadership, making it crucial for housing professionals to exude confidence and decisiveness. This doesn't mean being authoritarian but rather demonstrating a commanding knowledge of the field, especially concerning VA loans and veteran-specific housing needs.

UNDERSTANDING
VETERAN-SPECIFIC NEEDS

Veterans often have unique needs due to their service experiences. For instance, some might prioritize proximity to veteran medical facilities or look for communities with a strong veteran presence. Understanding these needs and being able to provide relevant solutions is crucial. This understanding goes beyond the surface; it requires a deep dive into the veteran's world, empathizing with their experiences, and recognizing the sacrifices they have made.

THE ROLE OF THE PROFESSIONAL IN LEADING AND SUPPORTING

A professional's role in this journey is twofold: to lead confidently and to offer unwavering support. Veterans appreciate when a professional can navigate the complexities of real estate transactions with expertise and guide them with a steady hand. This leadership instills confidence in the veteran that their interests are being understood and addressed competently. At the same time, providing support, especially in understanding and utilizing VA loan benefits, is vital. Veterans often need someone who can demystify the homebuying process, making it more accessible and less intimidating.

CREATING A TRUSTING RELATIONSHIP

The relationship between a veteran and a housing professional should be built on mutual trust and respect. This trust is earned through consistent, knowledgeable guidance and genuine advocacy for the veteran's needs. A professional who can create this trusting relationship will not only aid veterans in finding their ideal home but also in feeling valued and respected throughout the process.

In summary, serving veterans in the housing industry is about much more than transactions; it's about providing leadership, understanding, and unwavering support. It's about being the knowledgeable professional who can confidently guide them through the homebuying process while respecting and acknowledging their unique experiences and sacrifices. As professionals, our role is to ensure that veterans feel supported and valued, leading to successful outcomes that enrich their lives and honor their service to our nation.

CHAPTER 27:
Transformative Impact

In the journey of life, unexpected opportunities often arise that can alter the course of one's career and personal life. For me, the turning point came when I discovered a profound purpose in serving the veteran community through the VA home loan benefit. This newfound mission not only reshaped my professional trajectory but also enhanced my role as a husband and father.

Finding purpose is a pivotal moment that can bring clarity and direction to one's life. When I took a leap of faith to completely change my business model to serve veterans with the VA home loan benefit, it resonated deeply with my values.

The chance to give back to those who had sacrificed so much for our country ignited a sense of purpose that transcended everything. I realized that this endeavor had the potential to make a meaningful impact on the lives of veterans and their families, providing them with a pathway to homeownership.

When I decided to make that change, I was at a horrible point in my life. I was in a horrible state of depression and making very poor decisions that not only affected my business but my family. I finally had to confront those demons and begin the healing process. Embracing the mission of serving veterans through the VA home loan benefit led to a profound transformation in my life. Initially, my professional journey lacked a sense of purpose and joy, and I found myself at a crossroads. When I discovered who I really was I not only gained expertise in the field but also developed a passion for helping veterans navigate the complexities of their benefit. This newfound passion translated into a more rewarding and fulfilling career, aligning my professional endeavors with a very personal sense of purpose.

Working closely with veterans and their families provided me with a unique perspective on their challenges and aspirations. I never had the honor of serving my country. But my grandfathers, Father, and older Brother answered that call. The intricate process of securing a VA home loan unveiled the layers of sacrifice and dedication from their service. This exposure fostered a deep sense of empathy and understanding, sharpening my skills. As I assisted veterans in realizing their homeownership dreams, I learned to appreciate the resilience and determination that characterized their military service, further enriching my ability to connect with people on a personal level.

The transformation in my career didn't just impact my professional life; it also significantly improved my role as a husband. The empathy and understanding gained through serving the veteran community translated into a more compassionate and supportive approach at home. Recognizing the challenges faced by veterans and their families strengthened my commitment to creating a nurturing and understanding environment within my own family. I became more in tune with the needs of my spouse, fostering a deeper connection built on shared values and a mutual understanding of the importance of sacrifice and resilience.

The lessons learned through serving the veteran community spilled over into my role as a father. Instilling the values of service and sacrifice became a central theme in our family. Sharing stories of the veterans I had the pleasure of meeting, I aimed to impart a sense of gratitude and respect for the sacrifices made by those who protect our freedom. This not only contributed to the character development of my children but also reinforced the importance of service to others.

In the pursuit of a meaningful and fulfilling life, discovering a purpose that aligns with one's values can be life-changing. Serving the veteran community through the VA home loan benefit not only reshaped my career but also enhanced my role as a husband and father. The journey has been a testament to the impact that purpose-driven work can have on every aspect of one's life, leading to a more *rewarding existence*.

CHAPTER 28:
Education is Everything

I started in the mortgage industry in Feb of 2000. It took me all of two weeks to mess up my first deal. I had no training and there was zero test for licensing needed back then. All you had to do was pay for your license and you were a licensed originator. It seems silly as I think about it now. I was going to help people with the largest purchase of their lifetimes and there was no education needed.

Fast forward to today and there is a bigger barrier to entry and some licensing and education needed but most of the education is around compliance, rules and regulations. This is all important stuff mind you. It's just not the education that is going to help you structure a loan, run a break-even analysis or help you navigate the complexities of mortgage underwriting. Not even close.

Let's get back to my epic failure. I was working on a conventional cash out refinance and structured the loan at eighty five percent loan to value, waiving escrows because there wasn't enough room in the new loan amount to fit them in and the borrower preferred to not escrow. No Problem! Right? Well, if you have been originating for more than a few months you know. That's not allowed. If your loan is over eighty percent loan to value, you must have private mortgage insurance and escrow our taxes and insurance into your new loan. Oops.

I will just say this. The borrower did not give me a five-star Google review. The fact they didn't exist yet was a blessing in this case. I can still remember how embarrassed I was. It was a terrible feeling. Self-doubt settled in and I didn't think I was cut out for this industry.

Twenty-four years later and I am still thankful for that moment. It's because of that failure and the embarrassment that followed that fueled my journey on making sure it never happened again.

MASTERING YOUR CRAFT

The benefits of mastering your craft are endless. But so is the process. I am not going to promote or tell you where or how you need to get your education. This is going to be different for everyone based on many factors. Instead, I am going to focus on the benefits of the ongoing journey and the mindset needed to master your craft.

I love the saying "You don't know what you don't know". To me this means to always be open to learning, however the lesson comes to you. If you start to think or say you have it all mastered, you will soon find out this industry has a way of proving you wrong.

One of the best things mastering your craft will do is build confidence. When you have confidence, you portray it. You can answer questions with ease and People naturally want to work with someone who gives them the confidence that they can get the job done. Realtors want to work with a professional. They don't want to work with someone that's unsure of themselves or their abilities. Their reputation is on the line when referring a client to you. You must take that seriously and always make them feel like they are in good hands with you.

Here are a few more benefits to mastering your craft that will help fill your pipeline.

CONVERTING ANOTHER LENDERS TURNDOWN TO A CLOSED LOAN.

If you want to wow your Realtor partners have them send you transactions that fall through our another lender could not approve. You are not going to be able to save every deal but you would be surprised at how many people are falsely turned down for one reason or another. This also bring up the importance of knowing your competition. If another lender has an overlay that will hinder them from approving a buyer you can use that to your advantage. Once you convert a few loans to the closing table you will have earned the right to ask them to send them to you first so the customer has a better experience. Be patient. This can take time and you need to earn the trust and confidence of your future business partner.

MASTERING A SPECIALIZED LOAN PROGRAM TO SET YOURSELF APART.

There are so many opportunities that exist around this. Lets use a FHA 203k loan program for an example. Once you master the guidelines that help you navigate this loan program you can use is as your superpower. You can use it to educate Realtors to see how they can sell more homes. You can partner with a contractor and help educate his clients on the benefits and how to be able to afford that new kitchen they wanted. You can educate your current buyers that are having trouble finding a home through that process to make any house their dream home. If you are helping your partners build their business I can tell you from experience they will help you build yours. Now you can go teach this class to create a steady stream of business for you and your partners.

HELPS NAVIGATE CHALLENGES AS THEY COME UP TO CREATE A SMOOTH TRANSACTION.

The reality of this industry is there will always be unforeseen situations that can pop up during the process. This should be expected. When you are armed with the proper knowledge and resources your should be able to come up with a solution to overcome these quickly. Your other super power should be solving problems nobody even knew existed.

BE THE GUY / GAL.

You know. The one everyone thinks of when they have a mortgage question. Once you have established this in your market you are off to the races. Your goal should be to their go to person for all thing mortgage. Every call or text is another opportunity to build trust, strengthen the relationship and provide value. The rest will take care of itself.

SAY YES.

There is almost always a path to homeownership. Figure out what that looks like for each borrower and tell them yes. No matter how extreme it may be. It could be something like, I can get you preapproved once you pay off your $50,000 credit card debt, save up 25% down and wait another year at your current employer. You will be surprised at how many people find a way to make it happen. These borrowers also send referrals. Every other lender didn't call them back or simply denied their loan. You said yes and gave them a path.

LEVERAGING YOUR KNOWLEDGE

When Mortgage Nerds were born, we focused on all things' education. We built an entire brand around it. Our logo is a "cool" Nerd, our slogan is "Mortgages are complex. Let Mortgage Nerds give you the answers you need". My elevator speech is, I educate and empower people to use their mortgage as a tool to build wealth. It all works together. It works because I believe in it.

In the early days, education was centered around knowing guidelines and educating the consumer during the mortgage process. One Example of this is on every refinance transaction we partnered with a financial advisor and with the consumers permission we would send their potential monthly saving to the financial advisor and the consumer would receive a custom email with detailed quotes on what it would look like if they didn't pay any extra on their new mortgage payment and invested the money they saved each month instead.

Borrowers are usually shocked at the numbers. No matter what they decided to do in the future with their savings from the refinance I know they are better educated and have a better understanding of how to use a mortgage as a tool to build wealth. Hopefully we planted a seed for the future investor in them if they don't decide to do it today.

When we took the time to truly educate the borrower, they were impressed by it. We would hear them say things like why anyone hasn't else has ever told me this. How is this possible? Why wouldn't I do this? They were happy with the extra effort and their referrals proved that to us.

Our next step in education evolved into teaching classes. We started teaching first time home buyer classes and quickly realized we found "our thing". Educating and empowering people is what we are good at and enjoy doing. Our passion for it helps us connected to the audience.

Scan QR code to get tips and tricks to teach a successful class.

HERE ARE A FEW OF THE CLASSES
WE TEACH / TAUGHT:

The pitfalls of mortgage lending – We taught this to new Real Estate Agents. Local real estate brokerages would contact us when they had new hires. WE covered different loan programs and the nuances associated with them. Honestly, all agents should take this class.

First Time Home Buyers Class – First Time Home Buyers are full of bad information and lots of questions. They are the perfect audience to show off our ability.

First Time Home Buyer Class (Parent Addition) – This is the same class as above with a twist. Most first-time homebuyers are going to be influenced by their parents and their bad advice. Get them in the room and overcome their bad information in the class. Give a prize to just the parents who attend.

Bonus: Once Mom or Dad is on board you get the rest of the children's loans.

VA Myth Busting – We teach this class all over the state and on an Army Base in Wisconsin. We overcome all the bad information Veterans have been told by bad lenders, agents and other Veterans. This is our #1 class and aligns with our mission to help more Veterans. #VAIsBetter

How to use your Mortgage as a tool to build wealth – This covers the different options and strategies to build wealth in real estate.

When you stand in front of a room and educate people and answer their questions in a way that they can understand it will change the way they view you. You become the authority figure on that subject. When that happens, they will naturally want to do business with you. Don't we all want to work with someone we know, like and trust? Teaching should get you all three. If not, keep practicing.

DRIVING THE PROCESS: OWNERSHIP AND ACCOUNTABILITY

The role of a mortgage Professional extends beyond moving the file through your system to closing. It involves taking ownership of the entire process. This responsibility entails a thorough understanding of industry guidelines and the ability to navigate the challenges that arise. Whether addressing unnecessary conditions imposed by underwriters or rectifying mistakes, the onus is on us to ensure a seamless transaction. Embracing this level of accountability is crucial for not only advancing personal growth but also for maintaining the trust and confidence of clients and partners alike. I like the phrase "You drive the bus". Everyone else is along for the ride.

If for some reason you made a mistake, own it at once and learn from it. Use the pain as a motivator to ensure it doesn't happen again.

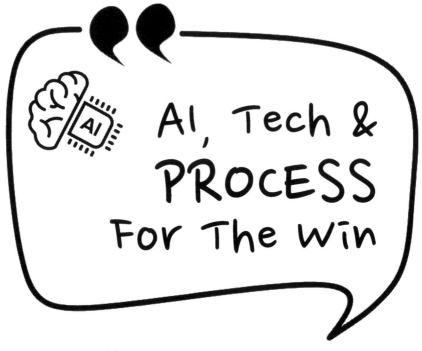

AI, Tech & PROCESS For The Win

Presented by:

shape

Shape is the only mortgage solution that combines an integrated CRM, dialer, email/text automation, POS, LOS integrations, pre-built CRO websites and more than 500 additional features within a single system. Finally.

Additionally, Shape seamlessly integrates with more than 5,000 applications, offering a smooth customer experience and increased productivity through its extensive marketing suite and lead management intelligence using AI.

You've made it to the final section of the book, here we will uncover the intricacies of modern mortgage lending, where technology intersects with deeply personal narratives, transforming the way we connect with borrowers and real estate partners alike. At the heart of this exploration lies a fundamental truth: every customer interaction carries immense significance, shaping not just financial transactions but the very fabric of families' lives.

You'll learn about lead management, where time is a precious commodity and prioritization becomes paramount. Through innovative CRM systems and strategic approaches, we unlock the potential to optimize every interaction, recognizing the power of personalized engagement in fostering lasting relationships.

Additionally, we encounter the transformative power of content creation, where AI technologies revolutionize the landscape, offering streamlined solutions for loan officers to craft compelling narratives and nurture connections. From leveraging AI prompts to mastering the art of personalized brand differentiation, we discover how technology becomes a catalyst for meaningful engagement. By redefining our approach to collaboration and offering genuine value, we unlock a wealth of referrals, reinforcing the notion that success in mortgage lending transcends mere transactions—it's about empowering dreams and forging bonds that endure. Together, these chapters form a roadmap to a new era of mortgage lending—one defined by empathy, innovation, and a relentless commitment to changing lives.

CHAPTER 29:
What is the LO System Of The Future?

The mortgage landscape has changed significantly in the past five years, propelled by technological innovation, evolving consumer data, and economic fluctuations. To navigate successfully, mortgage professionals must embrace a paradigm shift, placing relationship curation at the forefront with an unmatched, lifetime value proposition baked into all communications.

Gone are the days of grappling with multiple CRMs and myriad, gimmicky platforms. Originators now need to wield the most effective systems and integrate essential technology into their daily operations. The expectation for loan officer assistants to "handle tech" while originators focus on relationships can create havoc in the customer experience.

Mortgage teams must embrace the same technologies, ensuring each team member comprehends the platforms, eliminating confusion and duplicated messaging, and providing an outstanding customer experience.

Real estate professionals are also adapting, making 2024 the opportune time to establish clear expectations for future partnerships. While the foundation of referral relationships can take various forms, their sustained success hinges on authentic (though sometimes automated) relationship maintenance. Reciprocity becomes vital in the future. Originators must offer real estate agents co-branded opportunities, presenting the most compelling value proposition in the market and solidifying themselves as a team dedicated to serving leads and referrals today and for years to come.

MASTERING THE FUTURE:
10 STRATEGIES FOR THE 2024 MORTGAGE ORIGINATOR

1 **Enhance Customer Experience Through Technology:** Understand how technology can elevate the customer experience, making interactions seamless and efficient.

2 **Create Personalized Customer Journeys:** Craft customer journeys based on data, geography, and personalization — curating and segmenting databases for tailored communication.

3 **Adopt an Omni-Channel Strategy:**
Allow customers to connect across any device or platform flawlessly through SMS, email, chat, etc.

4 **Simplify the Loan Process:**
Advocate for a more simplified loan process, making it easier for clients to navigate and understand. Stop asking customers or agents to learn tech to partner with you.

5 **Focus on Future Value:**
Provide not only immediate but also future value in all communications, showcasing a commitment beyond the transaction.

6 **Rethink Agent Relationships:**
Reevaluate the importance of agent relationships, ensuring true reciprocity of leads through strategic segmentation and marketing.

7 **Co-Branded Opportunities:**
Impress agents with a compelling value proposition, encouraging them to co-brand and share databases for mutual marketing benefits.

8 **Revamp Events with QR Codes:**
Transform traditional events into engaging experiences using QR codes to drive traffic, followed by a thoughtful marketing plan.

9 **Outsource High-Level Communication:**
Identify areas where outsourcing high-level communication and marketing can enhance efficiency, especially during slower market periods.

10 **Teach Value Proposition:**
Educate team members on selling the value proposition effectively, ensuring a consistent and compelling message. Teammates and referral partners should be able to easily recite your value statement to encourage more sales.

The Evolving Landscape: The Technological Revolution and Its Advantages for Success

While AI technologies offer incredible advantages, effectively leveraging them for business growth presents challenges. Striking a balance between the efficiency of AI and the personalized touch of human interaction is equally central as creating systems that reflect your service commitments in channels that customers use.

Data and relationships will be the focus in 2024. Sales teams must emphasize the long-term value of the "mortgage planner" instead of the transactional loan originator relationship.

The key is to sell the concept of sustained value throughout the customer cycle, which cannot terminate once a loan is closed or denied. Leads should become loans at some point in the future, and closed loans should provide multiple opportunities for refinance based on data intelligence. Every person in the database should be an avatar with as much information as possible, and a strategy to close a loan should be deployed.

New technologies will profoundly influence the future of lending, but figuring out "how" these systems work together is the greater challenge. At the core of this new landscape is the curation of the loan originator's database. Data-guided decision making will be pivotal in selling to future clients. Integrating with data partners and understanding the intricacies of systems are just as important, as many tech vendors have access to the same or overlapping data, creating confusion.

Predictive analytics will play a decisive role in 2024. Personalized customer experiences, market trend analysis, and risk assessment will all be informed by advanced analytics. A powerful CRM system is essential, and the integration of cutting-edge solutions ensures originators have a comprehensive understanding of each client, facilitating more personalized and effective engagement.

"Automating the best intentions" of a loan officer is not only possible but a necessity to keep LOs in a sales and relationship position and away from performing mundane tasks.

change the Expectations of Realtor Relationships

2024 calls for a reevaluation of agent relationships. Hoping for referrals and paying for leads is no longer a viable strategy if systems for co-branded follow-up don't exist.

Agents seek more than routine loan updates; they want to ensure their brand promise aligns with the lender's ethos. Curated databases provide opportunities for reciprocity, where loan officers can become excellent referral partners using the leads and relationships that they have had well established for years.

 Imagine articulating this pitch to a potential agent: "We work collaboratively on your entire former database to energize people who had dreams of buying in the past while also using data intelligence tools to provide insight on when they will be buying in the future. Not only will you capture all repeat business, but as a partnership, we provide all past and future customers with the roadmap for making future equity decisions based on real data on when to buy and how to protect your home investment. The best part is that I don't need you to learn how to do this, I simply need you to trust that my goal is to help us close four more deals per month." That's the kind of value proposition that doesn't require the agent to understand numerous tech, marketing, and CRM platforms — but most assuredly allows you to give them simplified solutions for creating more business.

Defining the metrics of the past five years is crucial to starting this year off successfully:

- Analyze every closed loan to determine if it was self-generated versus referral-based.

- Sales and engagement strategies should be devised based on this data, fostering a collaborative approach with agents.

- Articulate a compelling value proposition that simplifies the agent's role while delivering significant business outcomes.

- Outline what collaboration looks like and have monthly defined goals for engagement.

- Stop replicating the same videos that every LO is doing with their agents. Find a way to create excitement around your partnership.

The Mortgage Originator of 2024: Innovation Is the Way Forward

As we venture into the next five years, the mortgage originator's role transcends mere deal closures. It involves navigating the complex intersection of technology, data, and marketing.

Equipping originators with the right skills, tools, and strategies positions them as trailblazers leading with innovation, customer-centricity, and a commitment to excellence. Work for a company that aligns with the future, or work on creating systems that support the future.

The mortgage originator of 2024 is visionary, embracing change and navigating the industry's constant flux. While building future tech may face budget constraints in the short term, empowering LOs with existing tools remains imperative.

The LO's competition is not tech; the true competition is the adaptable loan officer who utilizes tech tools and promises and delivers incredible value.

CHAPTER 30:
Artificial Intelligence

Why do ostriches put their head in the sand? Many believe it is to hide from reality. But the real reality is they're tending to their future generation by caring for their eggs. A loan officer I coach once told me, "I'd rather be an ostrich and stick my head in the sand than embrace technology, specifically AI, because what I'm doing today works." I'd argue that it's time to stick your head in Artificial Intelligence and tend to the next generation of your business.

Listen, I'm not talking about learning to code and becoming an engineer. Rather, I believe those who embrace technology in this very antiquated industry will survive. Because the hard truth is that artificial intelligence will ABSOLUTELY replace some roles within our industry.

AI has been around for a long-time folks – everyone is starting to talk about it this year because of the expansion of GENERATIVE artificial intelligence. Analytical AI has been used for decades. In fact, I represented one of the first analytical artificial intelligence software companies that was public facing in the United States at an early age in my software career. At the same time, Stephen Spielberg's movie "AI" had just hit the big screen. I remember watching this movie and being fascinated by David, the AI boy bot. David, having heard the story of Pinocchio, is convinced that if he finds the real Blue Fairy, his wish to become a real boy will be granted. He believes this transformation will allow him to be loved, feel love, and experience emotions.

What does David the AI Bot have to do with mortgages? Emotion. You see, we often forget buying a home is the most emotional purchase of people's lives. Why? Because of love. Maslow's hierarchy of needs clearly outlines our basic needs as humans, starting with physiological needs. Included in these is the need for SHELTER. Shelter is our home, where we celebrate life, mourn loss, and live out our days. To me, this is rooted in the desire for a safe life, which helps us exist in a space of love. What does Spielberg's movie teach us? That artificial intelligence can mimic human feelings, but it can't generate real human EMOTION. As my son once wrote in a school paper, emotion and feelings allow humans to live in a world full of color. So rather than fear AI taking over your seat, let's consider embracing artificial intelligence to be excellent, and continue to make the mortgage industry burst with the color of human emotion and connection.

Those of us that are exceptional in the mortgage industry emotionally connect with others quite easily. In fact, in this antiquated industry, we are taught to build relationships with partners and clients using emotion, but at the same time we are pushing files thru underwriting, printing out flyers, and making phone calls to share new product updates. Unfortunately, we aren't taught to be small business owners or CEOs and to look at our business wholistically. When I asked CEO friends of mine how they would define the most important daily pillars of their business, the answers were all consistent regardless if the company was a service-based or product-based business: marketing, operations, sales, and finance. However, mortgage originators take note, when I asked how these pillars stayed intact the answer was unanimously,

"people using TECHNOLOGY."

As the CEO of my business, I don't just work on my profit and loss, sales, marketing, or operations daily. I spend an equal amount of time learning about or implementing new technology, specifically artificial intelligence. Why? Because integrating aspects of AI-based solutions into my business creates opportunity. What do I mean about opportunity? Time! Artificial intelligence gives me SO MUCH MORE TIME, because AI can solve problems or do tasks FASTER than myself and my team can. In addition, AI helps stretch my limited resources and compensate for a smaller staff because it can either quickly help with or complete the business tasks. Let's break down our four pillars of business with examples of how AI can create opportunity.

Let's start with marketing, as it tends to be one most talked about in our industry. So ChatGPT, yes you all use it. Bravo! And if you don't, that's ok it's the easiest artificial intelligence LLM (large language model) interface to use. If you haven't used it yet, it is as simple as typing into the Google search bar and asking it a question or to edit writing. Don't be scared give it a try.

But wait, there are so many MORE marketing tools in the world of generative artificial intelligence. What about video editing? Easy peasy check out *CapCut*. Need a new headshot? Try *PhotoAI* – BAM looking good! What about a new logo or creative image? Go to *Looka's* AI-powered brand creator. How about a website? Give *LIMEcube* a try and get that blog page finally created with a few simple clicks.

Now let's move to something less sexy, how about operations? Those that know me, know I love a good process workflow.

Let's start with something simple, like task management. *Todo. is* will give your step-by-step to-do list based on a project you input. Wouldn't it be nice if someone could summarize all your important must knows on all your digital communication platforms – well this exists in a fun little AI tool called *UnRead AI*. How about making informed decisions about your business, try *Decision Note*. As a coach I'm often told "I wish I was better at time blocking." If that's you give *Motion* a try, it's one of my favorite AI tools I use.

How can AI help you sell more? What about language translation? Talk about casting a wider net, the world becomes your oyster! Here is one of mine - and no hablo español.

If you really want to stretch yourself, why not hire a virtual employee with *Olympia.chat*? This way, you can spend more time on sales calls. One of the easiest problems to solve in our process flow is carrying the client's story and those very important intake notes throughout the life of the loan. So why not use AI like *Airgram* so you can focus on the conversation and pass your notes onto your team. Ditch the pad and paper and use AI!

While you may or may not run a profit and loss for your business, the reality is we talk about finances all day long. There are financial AI tools to help your business, clients, and referral partners that might be of real value. Need a simple accounting solution? Check out *FlyFin*. What about the client who can't give you a year-to-date profit and loss?

Maybe you should suggest Truewind for bookkeeping. Or what about SparkReceipt as an expense management tool for the agents you work with?

Everyone cares about money, right? Some more than others but ultimately, I guarantee there isn't a day that you don't think about it at least once. Why? A brilliant financial advisor summarized it best "money is so important to us because it weaves within all aspects of our lives, which is why we think about it daily, whether you obsess about it or not." Like money, I would argue that in the tapestry of life and business, one of the most powerful strings that touches all aspects of our lives is technology. The powerful thread of technology now or in the future will use some model of artificial intelligence. This integrated AI STRING will be woven within your four pillars of business making you smarter, faster, and more effective at your job. Pull your head out of the sand and embrace AI. Become the most colorful, emotionally intelligent mortgage professional you can be by using AI in your business. Remember, those who incorporate AI into their business are the ones who will thrive with it… And if you don't believe me, theresanaiforthat.

CHAPTER 31:
AI Simplified

AI is one of the most exciting new technologies to come around in a very long time. And let's face it, it's cool. But I am challenging you to rethink the way you use AI. If you're like me when I first started dipping my toe into this new technology, you're probably experiencing less than 1% of what it's capable of.

"Give me 10 first-time homebuyer video topic ideas." Have you asked ChatGPT for a version of this? This is called a zero-shot prompt, and it's how most people use AI. When I first started using AI, I used it like a search engine. I asked questions. It gave me answers. I was impressed by how it responded like a person and not like a search engine.

1. **The First-Time Home Buyer's Checklist**: A step-by-step guide to the home buying process, from pre-approval to closing.
2. **Understanding Mortgages**: Explaining different types of mortgages and what first-time buyers need to know.
3. **Saving for Your First Home**: Tips on budgeting, saving for a down payment, and other financial preparations.
4. **Finding the Right Location**: How to research neighborhoods, schools, and local amenities that meet your needs.
5. **House Hunting Tips**: Strategies for effective house hunting, including how to work with real estate agents.
6. **Making an Offer**: The process of making an offer on a house, including negotiation tactics and what to expect.
7. **Home Inspections and Appraisals**: The importance of home inspections and appraisals, and how they affect the buying process.
8. **Closing the Deal**: A walkthrough of the closing process, explaining key terms and what to prepare for.
9. **Moving In**: Planning your move, from hiring movers to setting up utilities in your new home.
10. **Maintaining Your First Home**: Basic home maintenance tips and tricks for first-time homeowners.

This is how most people use AI, like a search engine. Today, I'm going to introduce you to the AI multiverse. One of AI's superpowers is the ability to "follow" your chain of thought. This means that once it gives you a response, you can ask it to elaborate, refine, or rephrase an answer, and it references the entire conversation to reframe its answer closer to what you're asking it to do.

Knowing that AI works this way, think about context first. You can "train" the AI by providing it with context first, then asking it to provide an output based on everything you've trained it on.

Here's an example. Let's say you want to write an article about house hacking. You can ask your favorite AI, like ChatGPT, to "write me a blog post about house hacking with owner-occupied units." AI actually knows a lot about mortgage topics, and you might be impressed with what it produces.

Now, keep in mind that this is what 97% of all loan officers are doing out there right now. Single shot prompts. Ask, and you shall receive. In the multiverse, we are going to train the AI first using multi-step prompting. Here's what it looks like.

First, use a setup prompt. Tell the AI how you want it to act. Maybe you want to write a blog post or article, so you ask it to "act like" an experienced financial copywriter in the mortgage industry who is an expert at Google's SEO best practices. Tell it who your audience is. In this case, it's millennial first-time homebuyers.

> `"Do not create output yet. Let me know you understand and are ready for the next prompt."`

This is one of the most common lines I include in most of my prompts, and it is an important part of training a chatbot using a multi-prompt approach. The AI should tell you what it thinks you are asking it to do and ask you for the next set of instructions.

I find that when I am using more complex, multi-step prompts, asking it to "let me know you understand" will actually tell me if I'm asking it the right questions or setting up the task the right way.

Next, go online and find one of the hundreds of blogs and articles written by millennials about the topic of buying an owner-occupied duplex using an FHA loan and renting out the non-occupied side.

Now that we've told the AI how we want it to act, we're going to give it context. Your next prompt would look something like this - "I am going to give you several house hacking articles that I want you to use to learn as much as you can about the topic."

What you're doing here is not only giving it context, but also perspective. Choose articles that you find to be a really smart or interesting take on the topic. Again, we're going to tell the AI not to create output yet, "let me know when you're ready for the next prompt."

You're going to simply copy and paste the articles into your chat thread. Follow each article with the "do not create output" line.

Feed it 2-3 (or more) articles that cover a specific or broad approach to the topic you're writing about.

Once you've told your chatbot how to act and given it some context that reflects the perspective you are taking, you're ready to write a unique, SEO-optimized blog post that scratches far below the surface of the topic that you're writing about.

Congratulations, you are now a citizen of the multi-prompt AI multiverse. Using this approach, you will find that your content will be deeper, more informative, unique, and captivating to the reader.

If this all sounds too complicated, I promise it's not. To help, I've recorded a video for you, walking you through this entire example step by step. You'll also get access to a free multi-prompt cheat sheet that you can copy, paste, and customize.

Scan the QR code for free instant access to these resources and more.

CHAPTER 32:
Rethink content creation

As a loan officer, you know that if you want to create a profitable and sustainable lending business, fostering and growing relationships is critical. We must focus on relationships instead of just transactions. To grow these relationships, consistent content creation, which adds value to your target audience, is vital for your survival.

Unfortunately, most loan officers would rather go to the dentist than spend time creating content. Content is hard, "I don't know what to talk about, I am not a great writer, I hate being on camera, I don't know how to create graphics," and the list goes on and on. You need to rethink content creation and how the power of AI can simplify your ability to create winning content consistently.

In the ever-evolving landscape of mortgage lending, technological advancements have reshaped the way today's modern loan officer engages with clients. As a recognized content creation specialist and published authority in demand generation, I've observed firsthand the paradigm shift driven by AI tools in revolutionizing the ease at which you can now create compelling content.

AI technology has emerged as a game-changer for mortgage loan officers, revolutionizing content creation and driving substantial pipeline growth. This chapter will delve into the significance of crafting an AI marketing tech stack (content creation engine) spotlighting essential tools such as: Grammarly, Chat GPT, Adcreative.ai, Riverside FM, Sintra, Opus Clips, and Adobe Stock Images, and harnessing the potential of ChatGPT for personalized brand differentiation to foster and grow your relationships.

THE EVOLVING LOAN OFFICER AI MARKETING TECH STACK

 As a loan officer you possess an array of sophisticated AI-powered tools meticulously designed to streamline your workflows and augment marketing initiatives.

In today's competitive landscape, a robust AI marketing tech stack empowers you to easily craft compelling content that resonates with your audience, consistently filling your pipeline. Let's explore the key components:

1 **Grammarly:** This AI-powered writing assistant ensures error-free and polished content, enhancing your credibility and professionalism.

2 **ChatGPT:** An innovative tool that goes beyond standard messaging, offering personalized interactions with potential borrowers. When customized effectively, it becomes a cornerstone for your brand differentiation.

3 **Adcreative.ai:** Leveraging AI-generated ad creatives streamlines the content creation process, producing visually appealing and impactful ads/graphics for the mortgage business.

4 **Sintra:** The ultimate AI companion for your work and life. Sintra provides comprehensive prompts for all aspects of your content creation assisting you in quickly and efficiently creating content for targeted marketing campaigns.

5 **Adobe Stock Images:** Access to a vast library of high-quality visuals ensures captivating and relevant imagery, enhancing the visual appeal of marketing materials.

6 **Riverside FM & Opusclips:** AI-powered video editing tools that enable you to produce professional-grade videos, engaging your audience through visually compelling content.

SIMPLIFY YOUR MORTGAGE MARKETING

To fully harness the potential of AI, you must integrate these powerful AI marketing tools. A unified approach leveraging these AI-driven resources can significantly increase engagement, lead generation, and borrower satisfaction.

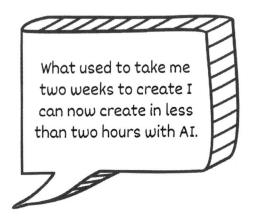

CHAT GPT: THE MAGIC CONTENT CREATION TOOL

Among these transformative AI tools, Chat GPT stands out as a cornerstone in AI-driven content creation. Its unparalleled capability to generate content reflective of your expertise and persona is nothing short of revolutionary. However, the true prowess of Chat GPT lies in crafting prompts that shape the quality and relevance of the generated content.

- Understanding Your Audience: Gather insights into your target audience's demographics, preferences, pain points, and aspirations.
- Crafting Unique Brand Voice: Develop a distinctive brand voice that aligns with your positioning statement, reflecting your expertise and empathy towards borrowers.

- Training ChatGPT: Feed ChatGPT with your brand-specific language, frequently asked questions, and unique value propositions, enabling it to generate personalized responses consistent with your brand's tone and messaging.

- Continuous Refinement: Regularly review and refine ChatGPT's responses to ensure they align with evolving market dynamics, maintaining relevance and authenticity.

THE POWER OF THE AI PROMPT

In ChatGPT, a prompt is the input or initial information provided to the AI to generate a response or continuation. Mastering prompts is crucial for achieving excellent results as they frame the context and guide the AI's understanding of the desired conversation or  content direction. Crafting effective prompts involves providing clear, concise, and relevant information, enabling ChatGPT to deliver more accurate, tailored, and insightful responses, thus enhancing the overall quality and relevance of the generated content. Understanding how to structure prompts optimally empowers you to harness ChatGPT's capabilities more effectively, ensuring more engaging, coherent, and valuable interactions or content outputs.

The modern loan officer that master's prompts will gain a significant competitive advantage, increased brand awareness, create more pipeline opportunities and close more loans. Once you have a strong understanding of prompts, if you really want to stand out from all other loan officers you MUST learn to personalize Chat GPT.

HOW TO PERSONALIZE CHATGPT

Personalizing ChatGPT is crucial for standing out amidst the competition and establishing a unique brand identity. Here are two ways to personalize Chat GPT with a step-by-step guide:

Option #1:
Craft a Compelling Personal Branding Statement

Prompt: "As a social media and content creation expert, create a personal branding statement for my mortgage loan officer business. I specialize in guiding borrowers to their dream homes by offering tailored mortgage financing solutions…"

Provide Chat with as much information as possible about your business, what makes you different, what are your hobbies, likes, your unique approach, background, dedication to clients, and expertise. This will culminate in a compelling personal branding statement.

Option #2:
Train Chat to Understand Your Business

Prompt: "Act as a social media and content creation expert. Before content creation, let's delve deeply into my business and audience. Ask relevant questions to craft impactful content."

This approach lays a robust foundation for comprehensive content creation by extracting essential insights about the loan officer's business, audience, and critical nuances necessary for crafting resonant content.

PERSONALIZING CHAT GPT USING YOUR CONTENT

Consistency remains paramount in effective communication. By consistently incorporating the personal branding statement provided, each subsequent prompt to Chat GPT mirrors your unique voice, resonating profoundly with your audience.

CONCLUSION

Gone are the days of stressing over content creation, the integration of AI technologies empowers you to easily craft compelling, personalized content that resonates with your audience, driving consistent pipeline growth. By leveraging an AI marketing tech stack and personalizing ChatGPT for brand differentiation, you can establish a strong digital presence and nurture lasting relationships with homebuyers on their journey to homeownership.

Receive a FREE copy of the Chat GPT Mortgage Cheat Sheet PDF:

CHAPTER 33:
Referrals > Leads

A referral occurs when someone recommends your business to another person. Leads come from your own marketing efforts to generate interest.

Referrals are better than leads.

We all know it.

I've been in the mortgage marketing and lead generation space for the last 20 years, and truth be told, that simple "business fact" always kind of drove me nuts.

It bothered me because, "I want more referrals!" was something I heard often, but felt powerless to do anything about.

It was deflating because 9 times out of 10, the excitement I'd sense when discussing referrals ran circles around anything related to digital marketing and lead gen...

Yet, I didn't have a solution to help my mortgage clients "get more referrals."

So my response was always a (somewhat flustered) version of, "Well then YOU need to do a better job of referring people business, and stop running around with your hand out and telling people how great you are."

(I wouldn't say it like a total jerk, but you get what I mean!)

So, for the longest time, to me, "getting more referrals" was simply a matter of giving first and finding ways to help others instead of just always being on the receiving end.

The idea of just being really good at what you do and constantly asking for referrals didn't seem like much of a strategy, either.

I still see it that way... but my "aha moment" came when I realized that digital marketing, lead generation, consumer direct marketing, and referrals are all INTERCONNECTED.

These things should NOT be compartmentalized and viewed as entirely separate from one another; instead, they should be fused together and used synergistically to strengthen the whole.

And based on that realization, a strategy and system could be developed to bring it all together.

 Scan the QR code to watch a quick video where I explain the interconnectedness of consumer direct marketing, lead generation, and referrals in more detail.

"88% of consumers say that they trust recommendations from people they know above all other forms of marketing messaging."

— Nielsen

Although that's probably not going to come as a surprise to anyone, let's focus on the operative word that makes referrals so powerful:

TRUST.

Trust is incredibly hard to earn (especially online and through marketing).

Referrals are a sort of shortcut to building trust because the foundation has already been established by another (already trusted) source.

Here are a few additional stats that show the value of referrals compared to other forms of customer acquisition.

"Referred customers can increase your profit margin by 25%."

— *Wharton School of Business*

"Referred customers' lifetime value is 16% higher than non-referred customers."

— *Wharton School of Business*

"Referred customers convert at a rate that's 30% higher than leads generated from other marketing channels."

— *Finances Online*

Identifying & Evaluating Referral Sources

Referrals from past clients, friends, and family are great, but they're limited.

What I mean is that these people are typically not in a position to refer business to you regularly, so the amount of referrals you can get from them usually isn't enough to keep your pipeline full year-round.

So, what other referral sources can we tap into that have the potential to consistently fill the gaps and produce even more opportunities?

If you guessed, "real estate agents!" — OK, I'll give you that.

Yes, good real estate agents can refer business to loan officers consistently.

But I want us to think BEYOND real estate agents and start looking at a much broader scope of business types and professionals as potential referral sources.

And once you identify a new potential referral partner, do some homework to evaluate key areas that can give you an idea of what type of partner you're potentially connecting with:

- Look for well-established local businesses in your area that serve a wide customer base. Search Google Maps and directories like Yelp sorted by most and most-highly reviewed

- Professional services like accountants, lawyers, and financial advisors are great since they have large networks to refer clients

- Home service businesses are ideal (plumbers, roofers, landscapers, etc.) as they have recurring business

- Strong social media presence, billboards, and check your physical "junk mail" weekly — if they're sending mailers and postcards (in other words: investing in their business!) these are all great signs of a good potential referral partner — put these folks at the top of your list to reach out ASAP.

What Makes Them Ideal:

Referrals from past clients, friends, and family are great, but they're limited.

- They already get a steady stream of customers. You want partners who are proven and popular, not unproven new businesses. This ensures they have clients to refer.

- They serve a broad demographic. For example, a roofer services all homeowners, not just a niche. Broad reach = more referrals.

- Some partners provide continuous or recurring services, not one-time transactions. This leads to ongoing relationships and repeated opportunities to get referrals.

One of my client's loan officers closed 8 VA loans from a pest control partner in just ONE MONTH; although that's not the norm, there's huge potential with each new business professional you connect with.

- They have a large existing customer base. You want partners who already have a trusted client network they can tap into to make introductions.

- They have incentives to refer business in complementary fields. A home remodeling contractor referring clients to a loan officer for financing benefits both trades.

- They are invested in the community. Local businesses with roots in the area are more motivated to connect clients to a trusted circle of quality local professionals.

- They already understand the value of referrals. Look for partners who actively ask for and make referrals. They'll embrace a relationship like this faster.

The ideal partner is already highly regarded, well-connected, and motivated to connect clients to other reputable local businesses that add value.

 Scan the QR code for a list of referral partner opportunities organized by Impact and Referral Frequency Potential.

Getting More Referral Partners: Understanding & Overcoming Challenges

While having a good reputation is important, it has limited influence when it comes to B2B referrals. If potential partners don't know you yet, your reputation won't matter as much since they won't have any personal experience with you.

(Yes, having a lot of great online reviews and a strong social media presence will help — they always do.)

To develop effective strategies for expanding and sustaining a robust network of referral partners, it's crucial to first understand the challenges involved. Here's a list that outlines some of these difficulties:

- No Unique Value Proposition (UVP)
- Good conversations fizzle out after a few days/ go nowhere — always starting over
- Shiny objects don't last — you need something truly valuable
- No connective tissue/nothing tangible
- Nothing consistently bringing value to the relationship (no effective "reminders")
- Hard to separate yourself from the competition (everyone's saying and offering the same thing)
- Approaching people with your hand out asking for business is hard and typically ineffective
- You can only REFER so many people that need X in any given month or year...

The question is:

How do we overcome these obstacles?

The Law of Reciprocity

The Law of Reciprocity is a psychological principle which states that humans have an inherent desire to give back or reciprocate when something is given to them, whether it's in the form of a gift, a service, or even an act of kindness.

What can you bring to new and existing relationships that creates ongoing value while keeping you top of mind (*while, of course, staying compliant*)?

creating a Trusted Referral Partner Ecosystem

In a nutshell: help spread the word about your referral partners.

Make it a point to help THEM get more business. The right partners will return the favor without you even having to ask.

In addition to proactively connecting clients and your network with trusted partners every chance you get, you can create value and stand out from the competition by:

- Building a "Trusted Local Pros" directory where you showcase trusted professionals across a variety of business verticals. Promote this directory in several ways, including but not limited to:

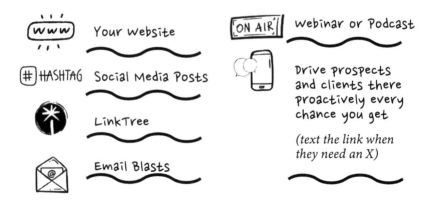

www Your website

 # HASHTAG Social Media Posts

LinkTree

Email Blasts

ON AIR Webinar or Podcast

Drive prospects and clients there proactively every chance you get

(text the link when they need an X)

- Featuring a "Business of the Month" spotlight where you highlight one of your partners and do some additional marketing to help promote them (social posts, email blasts, feature them on your website or office TV display, etc.)

- Featuring a local business each week in your email newsletter or social media channels. Give a special offer or discount code from that business to incentivize customers.

- Creating video testimonials for local businesses you work with and enjoy. Post them on your social channels.

- Writing great Google reviews and LinkedIn recommendations for your best partners.

- Co-hosting a lunch-and-learn or mixer at a local business, inviting your SOI. Have the business owner speak.

- Displaying brochures and cards for local businesses in your office waiting area.

- Sponsoring booths for trusted local businesses at relevant community events.

- Organize an annual local business fair and invite clients and contacts. Waive fees for trusted businesses to participate.

- Arranging client appreciation events at different local businesses on a rotating basis.

- Asking clients to share reviews and photos at businesses you refer them to via Google, Facebook, Yelp.

- Negotiating loyalty rewards or special discounts for your SOI from businesses you refer frequently.

- Placing signage/banners for local businesses at community events you sponsor.

Keep in mind, none of this can be done on the condition of, "You must send me referrals."

Yes, ultimately, that's what you aim to get out of it, but come from a place of wanting to help your clients and prospects connect with the best local businesses, and the rest will fall into place.

Scan the QR code to discover a specialized system designed to help loan officers expand their network and boost closed loans through referrals.

CHAPTER 34:
Digital Engagement

In the fast-paced realm of real estate, a fundamental principle has been the bedrock of my mortgage business: the loan officer who masters the art of communication invariably triumphs. This principle is even more pertinent today, as the real estate market becomes increasingly results-oriented and attention spans dwindle. In such a landscape, loan officers face two formidable challenges: comprehending their value and effectively communicating it to busy realtors and discerning consumers. This article sheds light on how loan officers can navigate these hurdles, significantly elevating their contribution to every transaction.

The Importance of conveying True value in Real Estate Transactions

In a world where results speak louder than promises, understanding and articulating actual value becomes paramount for a loan officer. It's about cutting through the noise with clarity and precision. The ability to swiftly and effectively communicate the correct information - not just any data - is crucial. Busy realtors and consumers demand concise, relevant, and beneficial communication that respects their time and attention. This is where the actual skill of a loan officer lies: not just in relaying information but in making it impactful, understandable, and tailored to the specific needs of realtors and their clients.

The Impact of Technology on Presenting value in a Limited Attention Span world

In today's fast-paced environment, where attention is scarce, technology becomes a critical ally for loan officers. A robust tech stack enables them to present complex financial solutions in a format that's both accessible and engaging. This is vital in addressing challenges like affordability, where clear and concise information can make a significant difference. Conversely, outdated or inadequate technology can hinder a loan officer's ability to effectively communicate value, losing a realtor's or client's attention in those crucial initial moments.

Digital offer - A Tool for clear, concise, and Effective communication

The digital offer exemplifies how technology can be leveraged to communicate value quickly and efficiently. It combines effective delivery with clear, concise communication, assembling all necessary components into an easily digestible format.

This method not only streamlines the decision-making process for listing agents and sellers but also aligns perfectly with the rapid-paced, results-oriented nature of the real estate market. Through examples in my presentation, I demonstrate how digital offers can be a game-changer in conveying value within a limited attention span.

Digital CMA: Tailoring Information to Realtor Preferences

Similarly, the digital Comparative Market Analysis (CMA) is a testament to how technology can present information in a manner preferred by realtors and sellers. More than just giving traditional data, it integrates problem-solving solutions, catering to the specific and evolving needs of the real estate market. For instance, it can offer strategic solutions for unexpected appraisal results or lowball offers, showcasing a loan officer's capacity to add value in complex scenarios, all within the preferred format and time constraints of busy real estate professionals.

The adept use of technology is instrumental for loan officers striving to stand out in a competitive, results-driven real estate market. By harnessing tools like digital offers and CMAs, they can effectively communicate actual value, respecting their audience's limited attention spans and preferences.

To witness the impact of these digital tools, I invite you to explore the QR code in my presentation. Experience firsthand the power of technology in transforming real estate transactions, enhancing communication, and elevating the role of loan officers in today's fast-moving market.

PERSONAL NOTE

As a mortgage advisor, I have experienced firsthand the challenges of conveying my value to the right people at the right time. Recognizing this gap, I took the initiative to create The Lender Marketing Platform.

This platform was born out of my journey and desire to enhance my ability to deliver and convey value and empower others in the mortgage industry. It's a testament to my commitment to bridging the communication gap and providing practical, technology-driven solutions for today's market challenges.

CHAPTER 35:

Unlock the Secret to Doubling Your REALTOR® Referrals:

Say Goodbye to Cold Calling, Chasing Agents, or Paying for Leads

How does working with real estate agents fit into a book largely about social media, consumer direct, online leads and being a "next generation" Loan Officer.

On average, four million homes are sold every year in the U.S. not including new home sales. According to the N.A.R. 89% of buyers use a real estate agent to purchase the home. A share that's steadily increased over the last decade.

That's a lot of buyers aggregated to a single source – **real estate agents.**

To ignore real estate agents as a viable source of business would be discarding the largest, single source of high converting buyers available for virtually no cost to you other than your time and effort.

On my Mortgage Marketing Radio Podcast, I've interviewed over 200 of America's top producing mortgage originators. When asked what their #1 source of funded loans is, 80% say "real estate agents".

Success Leaves Clues.

Working with real estate agents can have its challenges. Every lead source has its challenges. Most of the frustration with prospecting agents stems from one of the following:

1) Your Approach
2) Your Value
3) Your System

Let's take each of these and unpack them.

Your Approach

Most Loan Officers are trained to cold-call agents and lead with their products, pricing, and service. Gee that's unique and different, isn't it? No! It's the same lame approach real estate agents have heard on the daily for years.

When you lead with cold-calls, products, and pricing you're at the bottom of the pyramid, considered a solicitor or vendor. (See Figure 1, *REALTOR Prospecting* Pyramid)

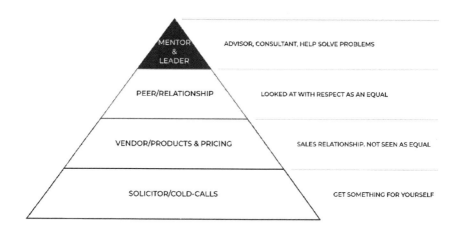

Figure 1: REALTOR Prospecting Pyramid

Do you want to be a seen as a solicitor and vendor? Of course not! If you want to be considered a "next generation" Loan Officer, you must stop selling and start helping. You must be considered a partner and peer.

How do you do that?

YOUR VALUE

Question: What is the primary challenge or obstacle you help real estate agents overcome?

See if you can answer this question without it being related to products, pricing, or service.

Challenging, isn't it?

I'm not saying that your products, pricing, or service are irrelevant. They are important. But they won't get the attention or engagement you're looking for when prospecting real estate agents.

If everyone leads with the same value proposition its value is diminished. Does that make sense?

HERE'S THE KEY:

If you want an agent's business you need to become part of their business.

How do you become part of their business? You position yourself as a resource, guide and facilitator of information and resources that helps agents solve relevant problems.

Try asking an agent this question during your next agent conversation:

> *"Hey [Agent Name], I'm curious, which of the following areas do you find challenging?"*

- Social Media
- Video
- Lead Generation/Conversion
- Technology
- Goal Setting
- Business Planning

You and I both know agents are seeking help in these areas and more.

How about *you*? Which of those topics do *you* find challenging?

If you're a "next generation" Loan Officer, you're likely struggling to learn or improve in similar areas as real estate agents are. You're reading this book which tells me you're on the right path.

YOU CAN BECOME PART OF THEIR BUSINESS!

You can be the resource, guide, and facilitator of information they are seeking. You don't need to be an expert. You just need to be a few steps ahead and be a guide along their journey.

What happens when you do that? You attract vs chase. You accelerate trust, expand your influence, and increase your referrals. Isn't that what you really want?

YOUR SYSTEM

The next generation agent prospecting process combines strategy, fundamentals, and digital tactics, into a unified system. It produces a personal brand of authority and influence, attracting vs chasing; propelling you to new heights of success with real estate agents.

The system at its core is teaching agent classes. Doesn't sound sexy I know. But stay with me just a moment.

ANSWER THESE QUESTIONS:

1. Do you want to reach more quality agents?
2. Do you want a compelling value proposition?
   (Not products/price/service)
3. Do you want more buyer referrals?
4. Do you want agents contacting you,
   vs you chasing them?
5. Do you want more income stability?

Leading with education is what moves you up the pyramid from solicitor and vendor to partner and peer.

What if you're value proposition was no longer about products/pricing/service? What if you simply helped agents learn alongside your journey as a "next generation" Loan Officer?

That was Part I. *Want to learn more?*

HERE'S WHAT YOU'LL GET IN PART II:

- Three Skills to Thrive in Any Market
- 5 Reasons Agents Don't Send You Referrals
- What the Top 1% Do to Get Agent Referrals
- The Agent Referral Blueprint Case Studies

"TOP-TIER ORIGINATORS AND BOTTOM-TIER ORIGINATORS HAVE ONE THING IN COMMON, THEY BOTH ONLY HAVE 24 HOURS IN A DAY. WHAT SEPARATES THE TWO IS HOW THEY USE THOSE 24 HOURS."
DALE VERMILLION

CHAPTER 36:
Every Lead Matters

Lead Management is very personal for me, but even after spending close to 20 years in this line of work, I really didn't know how personal it really was until just a few years ago. It's a hard story to fully explain via a chapter in this book, so I recorded a video that explains all the details of the situation. You can access this video by scanning this QR Code.

Long story short, my father at 33 years old (when I was 9 years old) made the unfortunate decision to end his own life and one of the contributing factors to his situation that I now know of, was not being able to qualify for a home purchase that he desperately wanted for his three boys after a difficult divorce from my mother.

I tell this story not to make people feel bad for me or my two younger brothers but to tell an important story to all of those reading this book - Every customer you interact with has a "Dream of Homeownership" story and every single customer matters.

So, to help those who are truly interested as a Loan Originator in changing family's lives with the gift of homeownership, I'm providing three tips that I've seen literally change the game for many successful Loan Originators. Following these three principles with your Lead Management/CRM game will not only help your customers' lives but you may also find that it helps you in your personal and family life as well. My hope is that all of you can set yourself up for success and help to improve every family situation for the better.

> "Top-tier originators and bottom-tier originators have one thing in common, they both only have 24 hours in a day. What separates the two is how they use those 24 hours."
>
> – Dale Vermillion

#1
PRIORITIZE

I'm a big time "let's back into the numbers" type of person. We all know that time in each day is limited. As Dale quotes, the difference between the top and bottom Loan Originators is how they use the time that they have. For those who work an eight-hour day, you only have 480 minutes in a workday.

That may sound like a lot on the surface but let's assume it currently takes you 10 minutes each time to check in with a customer or referral partner.

Given these numbers, the MAXIMUM number of customers or referral partners touch is only 48. And that's assuming that you had no distractions come up in between and are very easily able to move on from one conversation to the other. Given any number of distractions and interruptions, best case scenario, most of you will only be able to effectively reach out to 10-15 customers or partners in any given day. If you only have 10-15 interactions, you must be super effective on which ones those are.

That's where *Priorization* comes in. Some people are savvy enough to figure out how to do this on their own. But the majority of us need help to be able to do it consistently. That's where technology can come in to help make your lives easier.

The best Lead Management and CRM systems out there have a component of Prioritization built into their systems but only the best systems have it all built into their system providing a complete and consolidated Mortgage technology stack. When it's all built into one system, it can consider everything in a Loan Originator's day and prioritize accordingly, making sure that every interaction with customers or referral partners is optimized. If you need help finding a system that does all of this for you, please reach out to me directly and I can walk you through this more!

"when trust is established, everything will go well for you. But not just once, over and over again!"
— kyle Draper

#2
BE MEMORABLE!

In Kyle Draper's original book "Rethink Everything You Know About Social Media", he talks all about the true power of social media and why you should be turning the camera on every single day. The power of video and social media in your nurture strategies will pay dividends for your long-term success but the most successful Loan Originators can use additional powers of video technology by tracking customer engagement with their video. Having an easy way to understand what customers are engaged and not engaged with in your video content over time allows you to put the customer on a journey that is best fit for them.

For example, if you send a video to a customer out of a CRM like Shape, you can easily track if a video was watched and if so, how much of the video was watched. This data is then automatically pushed into your CRM so that your Sales prioritization lists are optimized by placing customers higher in the list if they are consistently engaged with your content. It's common sense that someone who sees me constantly on social media and is watching my content will surely have a better conversion rate than customers who are not engaged with my social media efforts.

Another special trick is to make sure that you leverage a field in your CRM that I like to call "Remember This". This is the data field in your system where you add all the personal things you've uncovered during all your rapport building sessions with customers and referral partners. Using this strategy will leave your customers amazed at the level of detail you've poured into building a relationship with them.

A good example I like to dream about is the Dallas Cowboys winning another Super Bowl someday. If I've made intentional efforts to track the favorite sports team of my customers and entered that data into a trackable field, I now have an easy way to search for this when the Cowboys do win the Super Bowl. I can then turn the camera on and send out personalized videos to each customer I've done business with in the past and celebrate a big (and long awaited!) accomplishment with one another.

"Stop overlooking your first step in the
process - the customer!"
- Anthony Gutierrez, CEO of Shape

#3
INSPECT WHAT YOU EXPECT!

Listen, I get it. Being a former Loan Officer myself, I know first-hand that it is very hard to nurture EVERY single customer that you need to. And it can seem very daunting for the average Loan Originator to even know where to start in setting up a long-term nurture strategy.

The easiest way that I've found is to create an on-going process of "secret shopping" yourself (or you can call it a "Lead Experience Screening" since "secret shopping" doesn't sound as nice).

I started doing this to myself during my time as VP of Sales-Marketing at Mr. Cooper and I found that it truly helped me sleep better at night knowing that all of the loose-ends in our sales strategy were tied together. It also helped reinforce to our sales teams on why using the technology the way they should really mattered and the visual timeline that I created off of each secret shop brought it all home for them.

To do this, imagine you're a potential customer and put a "lead" into your normal process. Look at every call, email and text that you receive and use the current data to draft what you would expect from someone you were using for your own personal mortgage. Do they look the same? I love the line – "Inspect what you expect"!

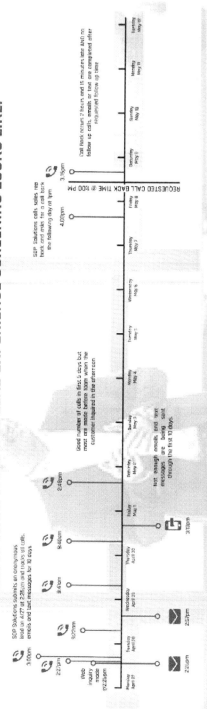

HERE IS WHAT A SAMPLE LEAD EXPERIENCE SCREENING LOOKS LIKE:

SDP Solutions submits an anonymous lead on 4/27 at 2:25pm and looks till calls, emails and text messages for 10 days

Good number of calls in first 6 days but none are made before 10am when the customer inquired in the afternoon

Not enough emails and text messages are being sent through the first 10 days

SDP Solutions calls sales rep back and asks for a call back the following day at 1pm

REQUESTED CALL BACK TIME @ 1:00 PM

Call Back occurs 2 hours and 15 minutes late AND no follow up calls, emails or text are completed after requested follow up time

PRE-CONTACT ANALYSIS

How many contact attempts are made?

How many communication channels are used?

What time are attempts made?

What is the quality of the communication?

POST-CONTACT ANALYSIS

What is the lead experience like after the lead connects with the rep?

Does the rep adhere to the lead's communication preferences?

Does the rep listen to the needs of the lead?

How does the rep continue to keep the lead engaged?

Put the results into a Timeline format like this

273

Simply looking at Day 1 to Day 15 is a great place to start. When would you expect phone calls? Texts? Emails? Map it out in a timeline and then use a CRM/Lead Management System (like Shape Software) to set up the automation of the experience that you desire for your customer. Test yourself every 90 days to find where gaps may have come into play and what changes need to be made given any changes in your markets.

Over the past few years there have been on-going rumblings that technology will replace the Loan Originator. It's a great discussion that sure does get a lot of people fired up but as we've seen time and time again, the best Loan Originators adapt these changes in technology to make their process and customer experience even stronger. My hope is that you're able to take some of these tips and tricks and find ways to adopt them into your long-term strategy.

Today could be a day that changes someone's life forever as you never know which customers you'll interact with. It may just be a struggling family with the American dream of Homeownership and your efforts today could have a lasting impact a family's future generations.

CHAPTER 37:
The Power of White Space

In the rapidly evolving landscape of the real estate mortgage industry, we must recognize that the role of a loan officer has undergone a profound transformation. The constant pressure to meet targets, generate new business, manage client relationships, and stay ahead of interest rate changes and market trends can easily lead to burnout and exhaustion. Also, the days are gone when success is solely measured by the hours worked or the labor exerted. We've transitioned from an industrial and manufacturing-driven society into a knowledge-based economy where the quality of our ideas, strategies, solutions, and the depth of our relationships reign supreme.

In this chapter, we'll explore how this shift has changed how we approach work as professionals and why creating white space in our lives is more critical (and valuable) than ever. We'll also look closely at strategies for crafting a balanced workday and the transformative impact of brief but consistent times of sabbatical.

FIRST, LET'S DEFINE "WHITE SPACE"

White space, in the context of a real estate mortgage professional, refers to intentional, unstructured time or gaps in our schedule that are purposefully left open for activities other than immediate work-related tasks. It's a period when we step back from the unending demands of our job, our daily routines, and ongoing commitments to create room for reflection, rejuvenation, and creative thinking. White space provides an opportunity to recharge, gain clarity, and focus on personal and professional relationships, ultimately enhancing our overall effectiveness and well-being in our careers. It is a concept aimed at achieving a balance between work and life, as well as fostering innovation, productivity as well as deeper, more genuine relationships with our clients and influencers.

FROM INDUSTRIAL TO KNOWLEDGE-BASED ECONOMY

In the many decades of the industrial era in the United States, personal success was often equated with the amount of physical labor one could endure. Factory workers put in long hours on assembly lines, and farmers toiled from dawn till dusk in the fields. Hard work and sheer effort were the driving forces behind progress and prosperity.

In this context, the equation was simple: Longer hours of hard work equaled greater output, and success was often a matter of survival. Today, we find ourselves in a vastly different landscape—the knowledge-based economy. True success is no longer solely determined by how hard we work or how many hours we put in. Instead, success is the result of the quality of our ideas, strategies, and solutions. Loan officers, like professionals in almost every other field, are compensated for their expertise, creativity, intentionality, and ability to provide valuable insights.

We are living in the Information Age, where data flows abundantly, and access to almost infinite information is at our fingertips. While this era has brought incredible advancements and opportunities, it has also increased the complexity of our lives. The stress caused by the constant influx of information, coupled with the rapid pace of change, is truly overwhelming.

THE TREMENDOUS VALUE OF WORKING LESS

White space, in this context, has become our most precious resource. More simply put, it offers a sanctuary of clarity amidst the noise and complexity of modern life. Intentional, unscheduled time during a workday allows us the ability to step back, detach from the continuous stream of data, and gain vital perspectives. White space enables us to process information, make sense of it, and distill it into valuable insights and strategies.

Creating white space in our workday isn't merely about taking breaks; it's about engaging in purposeful thought, consideration, and reflection. When we step away from the busyness of our tasks of an over-scheduled and over-committed business life, we can grant ourselves moments of solitude. These are times where the door is opened to deeper thinking and understanding. Remember, we are paid for the quality of the solutions and benefits we offer; not the number of hours we can mindlessly slave away.

ENHANCED DECISION-MAKING

In this knowledge-based economy, decision-making is a pivotal skill. Having a disciplined pattern of white space can provide us with the mental breathing room to assess options, weigh consequences, and make informed choices. It also allows us to consider the long-term implications of our decisions, ultimately leading to more successful outcomes.

It's also important for us all to acknowledge that innovation is the lifeblood of the modern loan professional. White space nurtures innovation by encouraging creative thinking and brainstorming. It's almost always during these moments of quiet reflection that breakthrough ideas emerge. Loan officers who embrace white space are better positioned to develop innovative solutions for their clients that set them apart in a competitive market.

Additionally, the ability to establish, build, and nurture relationships is paramount. White space allows us to invest time and energy in fostering meaningful connections with clients, colleagues, and mentors. Obviously, high-quality, and genuine relationships, not simple, rushed contacts, lead to valuable collaborations, opportunities and successfully funded loans.

Again, the complexity of modern life is often overwhelming, and can lead to stress and burnout. White space serves as a vital tool for managing these challenges and to navigating an over-committed and over-scheduled world.

This unscheduled time offers a respite from the demands of work and allows us to recharge both mentally and emotionally, leading to increased resilience.

BUT HOW DO I DO IT?

Let's be honest. Creating white space in our work schedules is incredibly challenging, especially in today's fast-paced and demanding professional environments. However, it is not only possible but essential for our well-being and long-term success. For access to an E-book featuring 105 insightful and detailed ideas about how to create whitespace in your workday, use the QR code here:

THRIVING IN CONFUSING TIMES

As a loan officer in the real estate mortgage industry, you are part of a dynamic and ever-changing landscape. Success in this knowledge-based economy hinges on your ability to adapt, innovate, and provide value through the quality of your ideas, strategies, and solutions.

Remember that we have transitioned from a society where hard work and long hours were the primary drivers of success to an era where thoughtful, strategic, and creative thinking reign supreme. Embracing white space in your life is not a choice or luxury. It is a necessity for thriving in our new reality of confusing times and high-velocity change.

Incorporating white space into our workday allows us to navigate the complexity of modern life with greater clarity and purpose. It empowers us to make well-informed decisions, foster innovation, build meaningful relationships, and manage stress effectively. By giving ourselves the true gift of white space, we position ourselves not only for success but also for a fulfilling and balanced professional journey in the ever-changing, real estate mortgage industry.

On behalf of both of us, Kyle and Brian, we extend our heartfelt thanks to each and every contributor who shared their wisdom and insights within these pages. Your expertise and stories are what truly bring this book to life. To our partners and sponsors, your support has been instrumental in bringing our vision to reality, enabling us to share these valuable lessons with a wider audience. Most importantly, to you, our readers, we hope this book serves as a beacon, guiding you towards success and fulfillment in your careers. May the knowledge you gain here not only enrich your professional journey but also inspire you to continuously seek growth, innovation, and excellence in all that you do. Thank you for allowing us to be a part of your journey.

check out the other book in the
RETHINK EVERYTHING series.

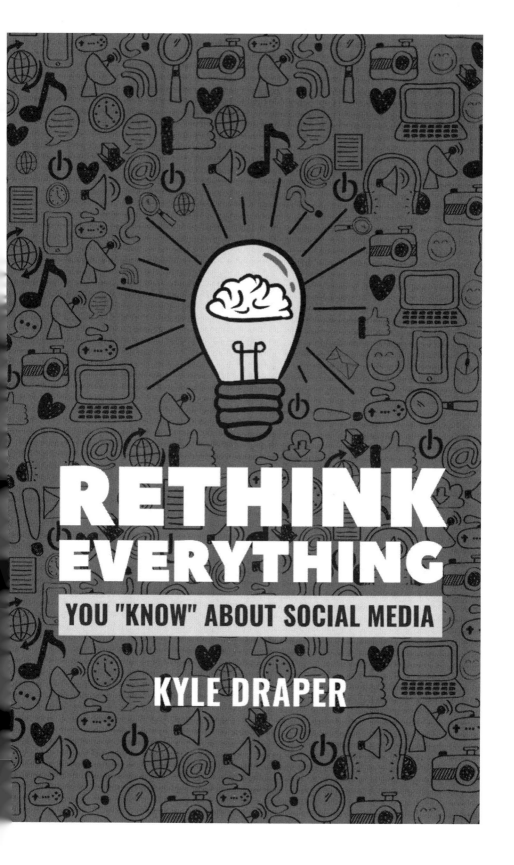

RETHINK
EVERYTHING

YOU "KNOW" ABOUT SOCIAL MEDIA

KYLE DRAPER

Made in the USA
Middletown, DE
25 August 2024

59125488R00159